NATEF Correlated Task Sheets

for

Automotive Electrical and Engine Performance

Seventh Edition

James D. Halderman

PEARSON

Boston Columbus Indianapolis New York San Francisco Hoboken
Amsterdam Cape Town Dubai London Madrid Milan Munich Paris Montreal Toronto
Delhi Mexico City Sao Paulo Sydney Hong Kong Seoul Singapore Taipei Tokyo

Editorial Director: Andrew Gilfillan
Program Manager: Holly Shufeldt
Project Manager: Rex Davidson
Editorial Assistant: Nancy Kesterson
Team Lead Project Manager: JoEllen Gohr
Team Lead Program Manager: Laura Weaver
Director of Marketing: David Gesell
Senior Marketing Assistant: Les Roberts
Procurement Specialist: Deidra M. Skahill
Media Project Manager: Noelle Chun
Media Project Coordinator: April Cleland
Cover Designer: Integra Software Services, Ltd.
Creative Director: Andrea Nix
Art Director: Diane Y. Ernsberger
Full-Service Project Management and Composition: Integra Software Services, Ltd.
Printer/Binder: LSC Communications
Cover Printer: LSC Communications

PEARSON

2 17

ISBN-10: 0-13-386651-3
ISBN-13: 978-0-13-386651-3

Table of Contents

We Support NATEF

Fire Extinguisher

Meets NATEF Task: Safety requirement for all eight areas.

Name ______________________ **Date** __________ **Time on Task** __________

Make/Model ______________________ **Year** __________ **Evaluation:** **4 3 2 1**

_____ **1.** Describe the location of the fire extinguishers in your building or shop and note the last inspection dates.

Type of Extinguisher	Location	Inspection Date

_____ **2.** Do any of the fire extinguishers need to be charged?

_____ Yes (which ones) ______________________________

_____ No

_____ **3.** Where can the fire extinguishers be recharged? List the name and telephone number of the company.

____

_____ **4.** What is the cost to recharge the fire extinguishers?

a. Water = ______________

b. CO_2 = ______________

c. Dry chemical = ______________

Vehicle Hoisting

Meets NATEF Task: Safety requirement for all eight areas.

Name ______________________________ **Date** __________ **Time on Task** __________

Make/Model ________________________ **Year** _________ **Evaluation: 4 3 2 1**

Getting Ready to Hoist the Vehicle

_____ **1.** Drive the vehicle into position to be hoisted (lifted) being certain to center the vehicle in the stall.

_____ **2.** Pull the vehicle forward until the front tire rests on the tire pad (if equipped).

_____ **3.** Place the gear selector into the park position (if the vehicle has an automatic transmission/transaxle) or in neutral (if the vehicle has a manual transmission/transaxle) and firmly apply the parking brake.

_____ **4.** Lower the driver's side window before exiting the vehicle. (This step helps prevent keys from being accidentally being locked in the vehicle.)

_____ **5.** Position the arms and hoist pads under the frame or pinch-weld seams of the body.

Hoisting the Vehicle

_____ **6.** Slowly raise the vehicle about one foot (30 cm) off the ground and check the stability of the vehicle by attempting to move the vehicle on the lift.

_____ **7.** If the vehicle is stable and all pads are properly positioned under the vehicle, continue hoisting the vehicle to the height needed.

NOTE: Best working conditions are at chest or elbow level.

_____ **8.** Be sure the safety latches have engaged before working under the vehicle.

Lowering the Vehicle

_____ **9.** To lower the vehicle, raise the hoist slightly, then release the safety latches.

_____ **10.** Lower the vehicle using the proper operating and safety release levers.

CAUTION: Do not look away while lowering the vehicle. One side of the vehicle could become stuck or something (or someone) could get under the vehicle.

_____ **11.** After lowering the hoist arms all the way to the floor, move the arms so that they will not be hit when the vehicle is driven out of the stall.

Safety Check

Meets NATEF Task: Safety requirement for all eight areas.

Name ______________________ **Date** __________ **Time on Task** __________

Make/Model ______________________ **Year** __________ **Evaluation: 4 3 2 1**

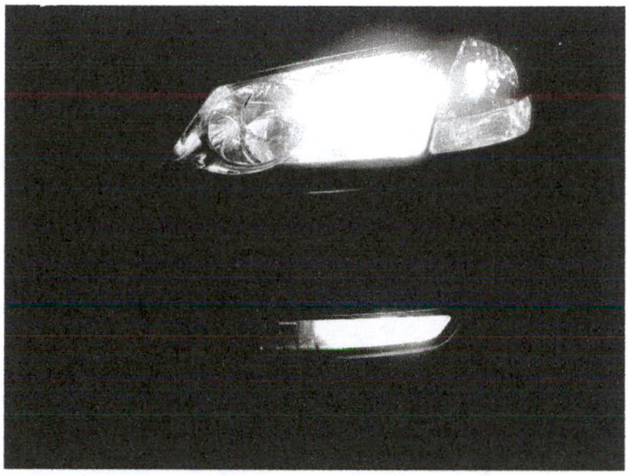

_____ **1.** Check the headlights (brights and dim).

_____ **2.** Check the taillights.

_____ **3.** Check the side marker lights.

_____ **4.** Check the license plate light.

_____ **5.** Check the brake lights.

_____ **6.** Check the turn signals.

_____ **7.** Check the back-up lights with the ignition on, engine off (KOEO) and the gear selector in reverse.

_____ **8.** Check the windshield wipers (all speeds) and wiper blades.

_____ **9.** Check the heater-defroster fan (all speeds).

_____ **10.** Check the condition of the tires (must have at least 2/32" of tread) and the tire pressure. Do not forget to check the spare tire!

_____ **11.** Check for looseness in the steering wheel (less than 2" of play).

_____ **12.** Check the 4-way emergency flashers.

_____ **13.** Check the horn.

_____ **14.** Listen for exhaust system leaks.

_____ **15.** Check the parking brake (maximum 8-10 "clicks" and should "hold" in drive).

Work Order

Meets NATEF Task: (A6-A-1) Complete work order. (P-1)

Name ______________________________ **Date** __________ **Time on Task** __________

Make/Model ________________________ **Year** _________ **Evaluation:** 4 3 2 1

Fill in the customer and vehicle information, plus the customer concerns and related service history.

UAS Automotive
1415 Any Street
City, State 99999

ASE CERTIFIED PROGRAM

Customer Information
Daytime ____________
Evening ____________
Name ______________________
Address ____________________
City __________ State _____ Zip ______

Vehicle Information
Year ______ Model ______________
Color ______ Mileage ______________
VIN ______________________

Materials

Customer Concern ______________________

Related Service History ______________________

Labor Performed ______________________

Root Cause of Problem ______________________

Customer Authorization

X ______________________

Totals

Materials ______
Labor ______
Misc. ______
Sub Total ______
Tax ______
TOTAL ______

Vehicle Service Information

Meets NATEF Task: (A6-A-1) Research the vehicle and service information, vehicle history and TSBs. (P-1)

Name ______________________ **Date** __________ **Time on Task** __________

Make/Model ______________________ **Year** __________ **Evaluation: 4 3 2 1**

_____ **1.** Vehicle and/or related technical service bulletins (TSBs).

A. Topic ____________ Bulletin number ____________
Problem/correction ______________________

B. Topic ____________ Bulletin number ____________
Problem/correction ______________________

C. Topic ____________ Bulletin number ____________
Problem/correction ______________________

D. Topic ____________ Bulletin number ____________
Problem/correction ______________________

_____ **2.** Vehicle history of repair. List all related repairs from customer records or repair order files.

____

____

_____ **3.** List all service precautions as published in service information.

A. ______________ E. ______________

B. ______________ F. ______________

C. ______________ G. ______________

D. ______________ H. ______________

Vehicle Service History

Meets NATEF Task: (A6-A-1) Research vehicle service information, vehicle service history and TSBs. (P-1)

Name ______________________ **Date** __________ **Time on Task** __________

Make/Model ______________________ **Year** __________ **Evaluation: 4 3 2 1**

_____ **1.** Search vehicle history (check all that apply).

____ Computerized data base (electronic file if previous service work)

____ Files (hard copy of previous service work)

____ Customer information (verbal)

____ Other (describe) ______________________________

_____ **2.** What related repairs have been performed in this vehicle?

____

____

____

_____ **3.** From the information obtained, has the vehicle been serviced regularly?

____ Yes (describe the service intervals) ______________________________

____

____

____ No (why?) ______________________________

____

_____ **4.** Based on the service history information, is the service record helpful? Why or why not? ______________________________

____

____

Technical Service Bulletins

Meets NATEF Task: (A6-A-1) Research vehicle service information, vehicle service history and TSBs. (P-1)

Name ______________________ **Date** __________ **Time on Task** __________

Make/Model ______________________ **Year** _________ **Evaluation: 4 3 2 1**

_____ **1.** Technical service bulletins can be accessed through (check all that apply):

____ Internet site(s), specify ______________________________

____ Paper bulletins, specify source ______________________________

____ CD ROM bulletins, specify source ______________________________

____ Other (describe) ______________________________

_____ **2.** List all related technical service bulletins that pertain to the vehicle being serviced.

Number	**Description/Correction**
____________	______________________________
____________	______________________________
____________	______________________________
____________	______________________________

_____ **3.** Based on this research, is the information located helpful?

____ Yes, why? ______________________________

____ No, why not? ______________________________

We Support NATEF

VIN Code

Meets NATEF Task: (A6-A-1) Locate and interpret vehicle identification numbers. (P-1)

Name ________________ **Date** __________ **Time on Task** __________

Make/Model ________________ **Year** __________ **Evaluation:** 4 3 2 1

VIN Number ________________

- The first number or letter designates the **country of origin** = ____________

1 = United States	6 = Australia	L = China	V = France
2 = Canada	8 = Argentina	R = Taiwan	W = Germany
3 = Mexico	9 = Brazil	S = England	X = Russia
4 = United States	J = Japan	T = Czechoslovakia	Y = Sweden
5 = United States	K = Korea	U = Romania	Z = Italy

- The model of the vehicle is commonly the fourth or fifth character. **Model?** _______
- The eighth character is often the engine code. (Some engines cannot be determined by the VIN number.) **Engine code:** ________________
- The tenth character represents the year on all vehicles. See the following chart.

VIN Year Chart (The pattern repeats every 30 years.) **Year?** ______________

A = 1980/2010	J = 1988/2018	T = 1996/2026	4 = 2004/2034
B = 1981/2011	K = 1989/2019	V = 1997/2027	5 = 2005/2035
C = 1982/2012	L = 1990/2020	W = 1998/2028	6 = 2006/2036
D = 1983/2013	M = 1991/2021	X = 1999/2029	7 = 2007/2037
E = 1984/2014	N = 1992/2022	Y = 2000/2030	8 = 2008/2038
F = 1985/2015	P = 1993/2023	1 = 2001/2031	9 = 2009/2039
G = 1986/2016	R = 1994/2024	2 = 2002/2032	
H = 1987/2017	S = 1995/2025	3 = 2003/2033	

We Support NATEF

Vehicle Safety Certification Label

Meets NATEF Task: (A6-A-1) Locate and interpret vehicle and major component identification numbers. (P-1)

Name ______________________ **Date** __________ **Time on Task** __________

Make/Model ______________________ **Year** __________ **Evaluation: 4 3 2 1**

_____ **1.** Describe the location of the Vehicle Safety Certification Label (usually located on the driver's side pillar post).

____

GM
MFD BY GENERAL MOTORS OF CANADA LTD.
DATE
06/02
GVWR
2071 KG
4565 LB
GAWR FRT
1115 KG
2458 LB
GAWR RR
956 KG
2107 LB
THIS VEHICLE CONFORMS TO ALL APPLICABLE U.S. FEDERAL MOTOR VEHICLE SAFETY, BUMPER, AND THEFT PREVENTION STANDARDS IN EFFECT ON THE DATE OF MANUFACTURE SHOWN ABOVE.
2G1WF52E839104270
TYPE: PASS CAR

_____ **2.** What is the month and year the vehicle was manufactured?

Month = ______________

Year = __________

_____ **3.** What is the gross vehicle weight rating (GVWR)?

____

_____ **4.** What is the gross axle weight rating (GAWR)?

____

_____ **5.** Is the exact date of manufacture listed on the label?

____ Yes Month = __________ Day = __________ Year = ________

____ No

High-Voltage Circuits Identification

Meets NATEF Task: (A6-B-7) Identify high-voltage circuits of electric or hybrid vehicles. (P-3)

Name ______________________________ **Date** __________ **Time on Task** __________

Make/Model ________________________ **Year** _________ **Evaluation: 4 3 2 1**

_____ **1.** Look for orange conduit and connections. This color indicates high voltage that could be fatal if touched. Describe the location of all orange-colored wires:

a. ______________________

b. ______________________

c. ______________________

d. ______________________

e. ______________________

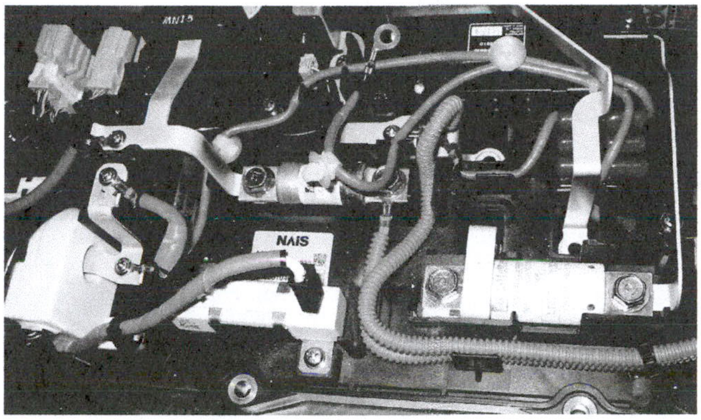
NAIS

_____ **2.** Most vehicle manufacturers recommend the use of rubber linesman gloves if working around high-voltage circuits. Research service information and determine when these gloves are needed to be used.

____

____

____

____

____

____

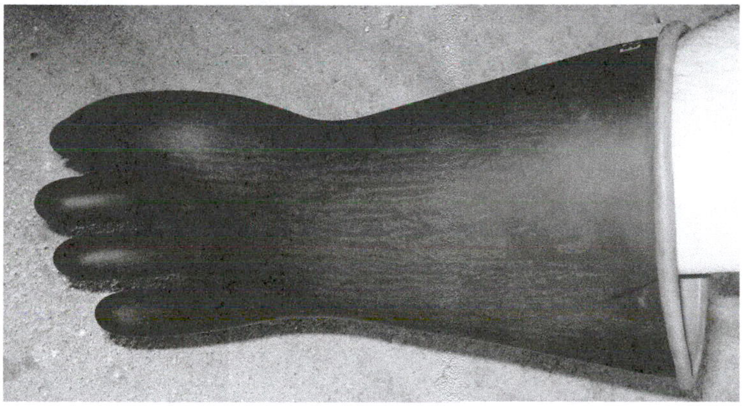

_____ **3.** What are the safety precautions listed in service information? ____________________

____

Hybrid High-Voltage Disconnect

Meets NATEF Task: (A6-B-7) Identify the location of hybrid vehicle safety disconnect location and safety procedures. (P-3)

Name ______________________ **Date** __________ **Time on Task** __________

Make/Model ______________________ **Year** __________ **Evaluation:** 4 3 2 1

Hybrid electric vehicles (HEV) use a high-voltage battery pack and an electric motor(s) to help propel the vehicle. To safely work around a hybrid electric vehicle, the high-voltage (HV) battery and circuits should be shut off following these steps:

Step 1 Turn off the ignition key (if equipped) and remove the key from the ignition switch.

Step 2 Disconnect the high-voltage circuits.

CAUTION: Some vehicle manufacturers specify that rubber insulated lineman's gloves be used whenever working around the high-voltage circuits to prevent the danger of electrical shock.

Toyota Prius
The cutoff switch is located in the trunk. To gain access, remove three clips holding the upper left portion of the trunk side cover. To disconnect the high-voltage system, pull the orange handled plug while wearing insulated rubber lineman's gloves.

Ford Escape
The high-voltage shut off switch is located in the rear of the vehicle under the right side carpet.

Honda Civic
To totally disable the high-voltage system on a Honda Civic, remove the main fuse (labeled number 1) from the driver's side underhood fuse panel.

Chevrolet/GMC Pickup Truck
The high-voltage shut off switch is located under the rear passenger seat. Remove the cover marked "energy storage box" and turn the green service disconnect switch to the horizontal position to turn off the high-voltage circuits.

Temporary Disabling of an Airbag

Meets NATEF Task: (A6-H-5) Disarm and enable the airbag system for vehicle service. (P-1)

Name ______________________________ **Date** __________ **Time on Task** __________

Make/Model ________________________ **Year** __________ **Evaluation: 4 3 2 1**

To safely work on the steering system of any vehicle that is equipped with an airbag (supplemental restraint system [SRS] or supplemental inflatable restraints [SIR]), it is important that the airbag(s) be temporarily disabled and reconnected after the steering service work has been performed.

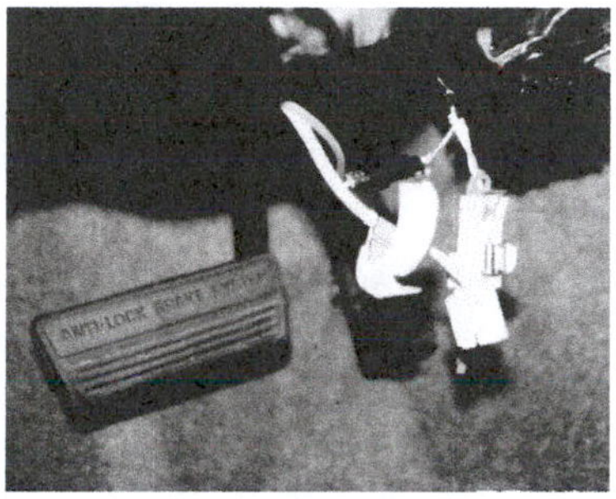

_____ **1.** Disconnect the negative (-) terminal of the battery.

_____ **2.** Locate and remove the fuse for the airbags.

HINT: The fuse for the airbag(s) often has a yellow band around the fuse to identify the airbag fuse.

_____ **3.** How was the specific fuse labeled that needed to be removed to disable the airbag?

____

_____ **4.** Disconnect the yellow electrical connector at the base of the steering column to open the circuit to the driver's side airbag.

CAUTION: This is an important step. The airbag could be deployed even without battery power, because the airbag computer module contains a capacitor that can trigger the airbag in the event that power is lost during an accident.

_____ **5.** Disconnect the connector for the passenger's side airbag (if equipped).

Location of the connector ______________________________________

Instructor's OK __________________________

_____ **6.** After all service work has been completed on the vehicle, restore the operation of the airbag(s) by reconnecting the electrical connectors and installing the airbag fuse and the battery connections.

_____ **7.** Start the engine and verify proper operation of the dashboard airbag warning light.

We Support NATEF

Material Safety Data Sheet (MSDS)

Meets NATEF Task: Environmental safety practices for all eight areas.

Name ______________________ **Date** __________ **Time on Task** __________

Make/Model ______________________ **Year** __________ **Evaluation: 4 3 2 1**

_____ **1.** Locate the MSDS sheets and describe their location

____

____

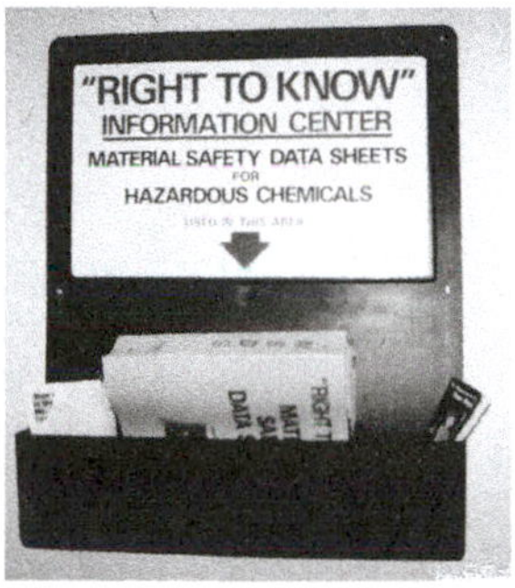
"RIGHT TO KNOW"
INFORMATION CENTER
MATERIAL SAFETY DATA SHEETS
FOR
HAZARDOUS CHEMICALS

- **Product name** ____

  chemical name(s)

  ____

  Does the chemical contain "chlor" or "fluor" which may indicate hazardous materials? **Yes** _____ **No** _____

  flash point = _________ (hopefully above 140° F)

  pH ________ (7 = neutral, higher than 7 = caustic (base), lower than 7 = acid)

- **Product name** ____

  chemical name(s) ____

  Does the chemical contain "chlor" or "fluor" which may indicate hazardous materials? **Yes** _____ **No** _____

  flash point = _________ (hopefully above 140° F)

  pH ________ (7 = neutral, higher than 7 = caustic (base), lower than 7 = acid)

- **Product name** ____

  chemical name(s) ____

  Does the chemical contain "chlor" or "fluor" which may indicate hazardous materials? **Yes** _____ **No** _____

  flash point = _________ (hopefully above 140° F)

  pH ________ (7 = neutral, higher than 7 = caustic (base), lower than 7 = acid)

We Support NATEF

Electrical Fundamentals

Meets NATEF Task: Not specified by NATEF

Name ______________________ **Date** __________ **Time on Task** __________

Make/Model ______________________ **Year** __________ **Evaluation:** **4 3 2 1**

_____ **1.** State the relationship among volts, amperes, and ohms.

____

____

____

_____ **2.** List five sources of electricity.

a. ______________________________

b. ______________________________

c. ______________________________

d. ______________________________

e. ______________________________

_____ **3.** Describe what occurs to resistance when:

a. The conductor length is increased ______________________

b. The conductor diameter is increased ______________________

c. The temperature of the conductor is increased ______________________

_____ **4.** What is the difference between a rheostat and a potentiometer? ______________

____

____

Electrical Circuits

Meets NATEF Task: Not specified by NATEF

Name ______________________ **Date** __________ **Time on Task** __________

Make/Model ______________________ **Year** __________ **Evaluation:** **4 3 2 1**

_____ **1.** Draw a complete electrical circuit and label all of the parts.

_____ **2.** What is an open circuit? ____

____

_____ **3.** Describe the difference between a short-to-voltage and a short-to-ground. __________

____

____

_____ **4.** State Ohm's Law ____

____

_____ **5.** State Watt's Law ____

____

Series Circuit Worksheet #1

Meets NATEF Task: (A6-A-2) Diagnose electrical/electronic integrity for series, parallel, and series-parallel circuits using principles of electricity. (Ohm's Law).

Name ______________________ **Date** __________ **Time on Task** __________

Make/Model ______________________ **Year** __________ **Evaluation: 4 3 2 1**

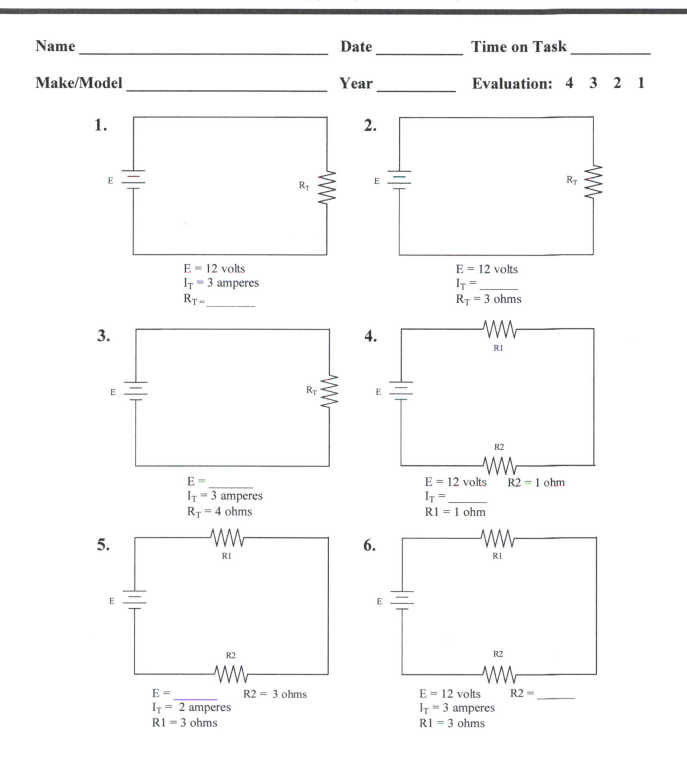

1.

E
R_T

E = 12 volts
I_T = 3 amperes
R_T = ________

2.

E
R_T

E = 12 volts
I_T = ______
R_T = 3 ohms

3.

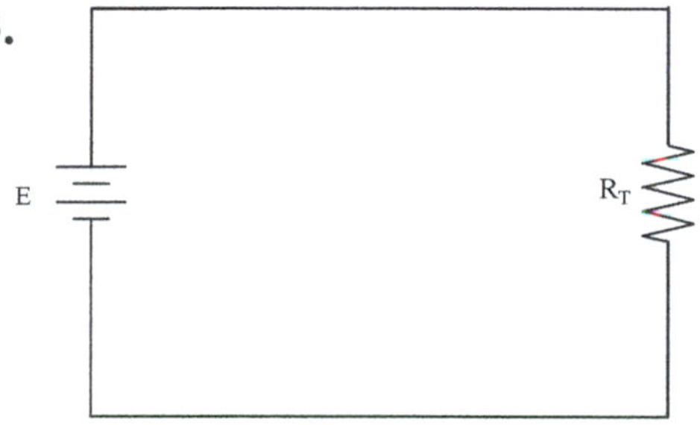
E
R_T

E = ______
I_T = 3 amperes
R_T = 4 ohms

4.

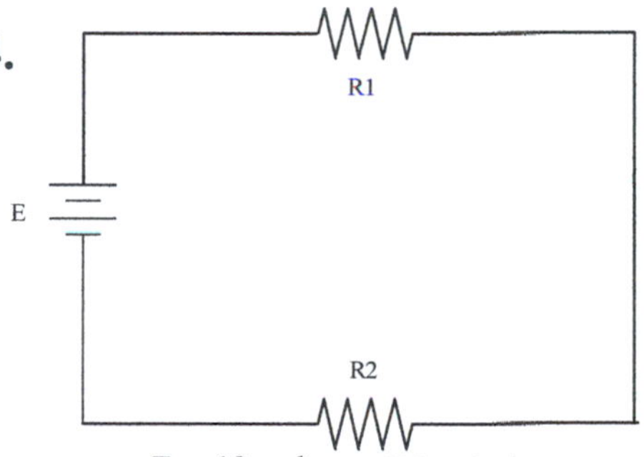
R1
E
R2

E = 12 volts R2 = 1 ohm
I_T = ______
R1 = 1 ohm

5.

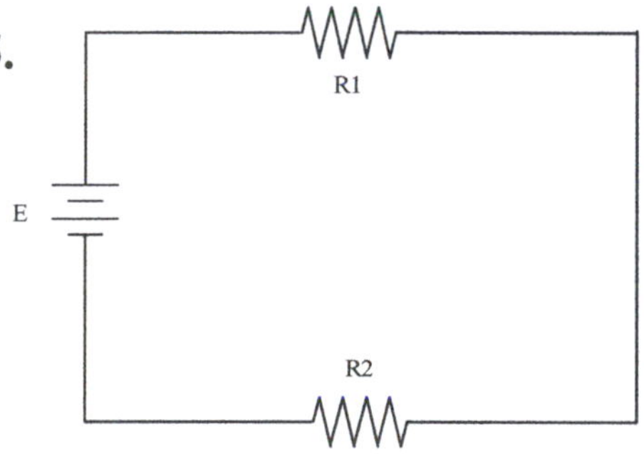
R1
E
R2

E = ______ R2 = 3 ohms
I_T = 2 amperes
R1 = 3 ohms

6.

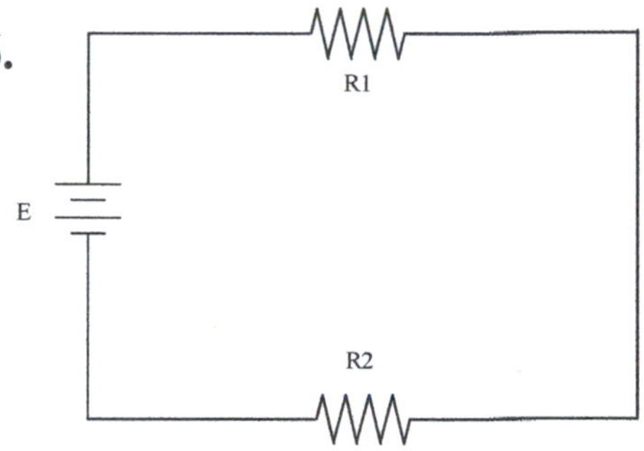
R1
E
R2

E = 12 volts R2 = ______
I_T = 3 amperes
R1 = 3 ohms

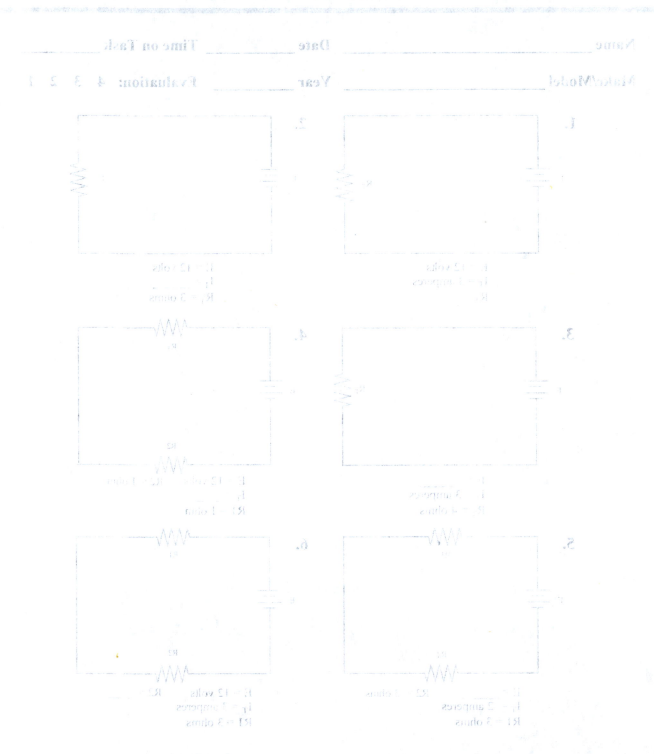

We Support NATEF

Series Circuit Worksheet #2

Meets NATEF Task: (A6-A-2) Diagnose electrical/electronic integrity for series, parallel, and series-parallel circuits using principles of electricity. (Ohm's Law).

Name ______________________ **Date** __________ **Time on Task** __________

Make/Model ______________________ **Year** __________ **Evaluation: 4 3 2 1**

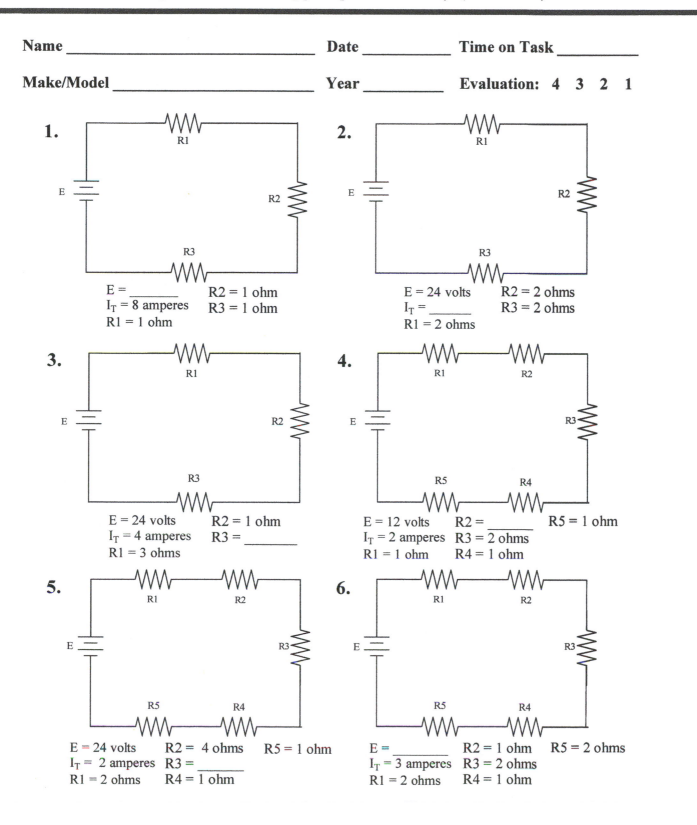

1.

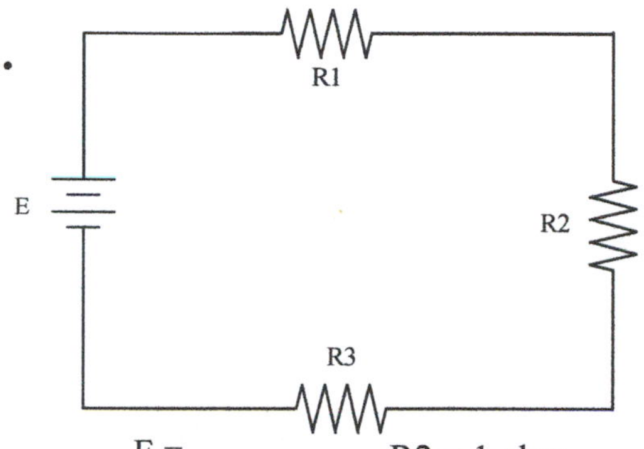
R1
E
R2
R3

E = _______
I_T = 8 amperes
R1 = 1 ohm
R2 = 1 ohm
R3 = 1 ohm

2.

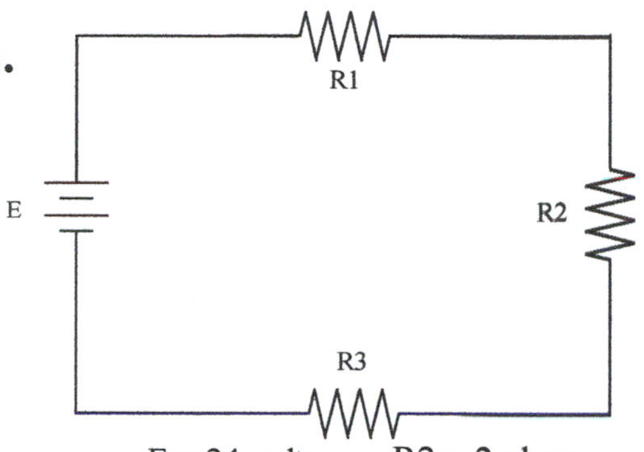
R1
E
R2
R3

E = 24 volts
I_T = _______
R1 = 2 ohms
R2 = 2 ohms
R3 = 2 ohms

3.

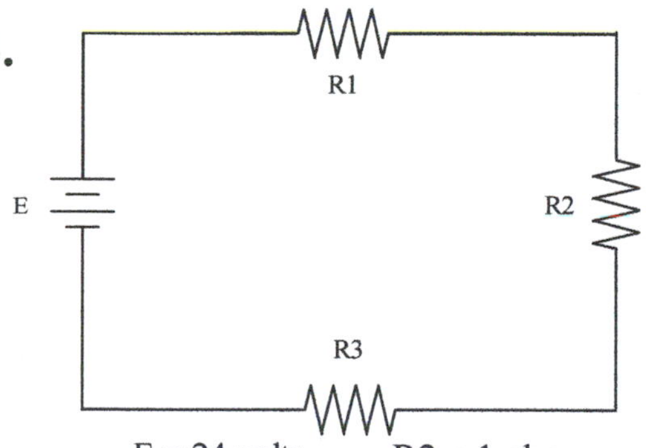
R1
E
R2
R3

E = 24 volts
I_T = 4 amperes
R1 = 3 ohms
R2 = 1 ohm
R3 = _______

4.

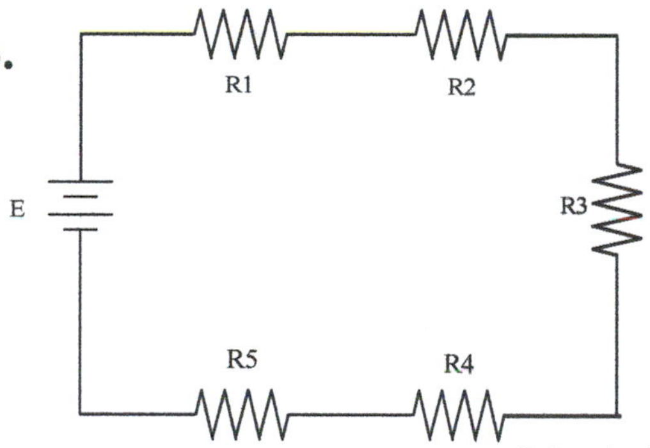
R1
R2
E
R3
R5
R4

E = 12 volts
I_T = 2 amperes
R1 = 1 ohm
R2 = _______
R3 = 2 ohms
R4 = 1 ohm
R5 = 1 ohm

5.

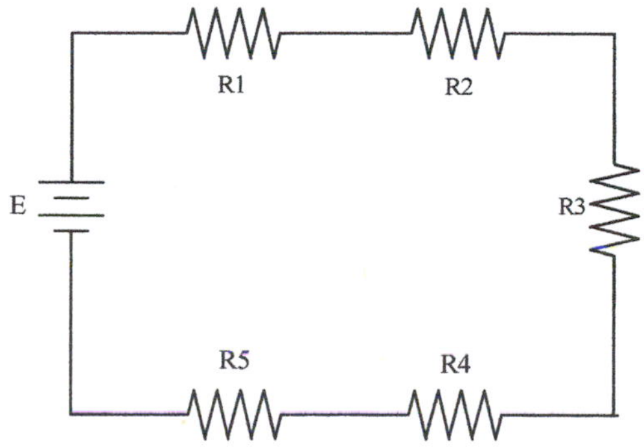
R1
R2
E
R3
R5
R4

E = 24 volts
I_T = 2 amperes
R1 = 2 ohms
R2 = 4 ohms
R3 = _______
R4 = 1 ohm
R5 = 1 ohm

6.

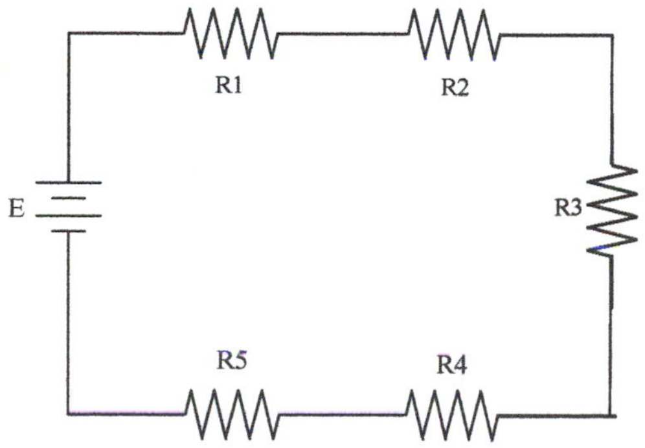
R1
R2
E
R3
R5
R4

E = _______
I_T = 3 amperes
R1 = 2 ohms
R2 = 1 ohm
R3 = 2 ohms
R4 = 1 ohm
R5 = 2 ohms

Series Circuit Worksheet #3

Meets NATEF Task: (A6-A-2) Diagnose Electrical/Electronic Integrity for Series, Parallel, and Series-Parallel Circuits Using Principles of Electricity (Ohm's Law).

Name ______________________ **Date** __________ **Time on Task** __________

Make/Model ______________________ **Year** __________ **Evaluation: 4 3 2 1**

1.

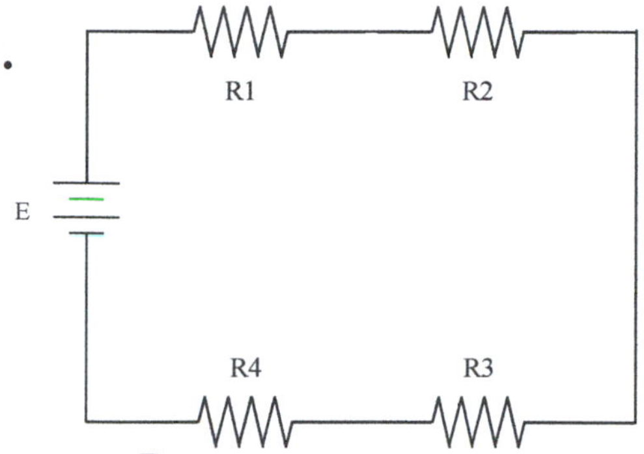
R1
R2
E
R4
R3

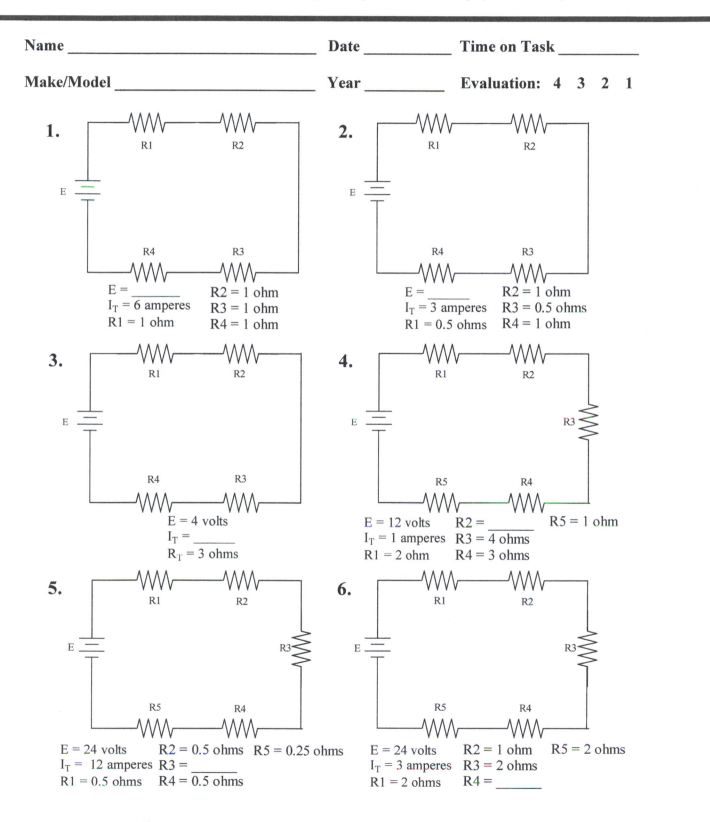

E = ______
I_T = 6 amperes
R1 = 1 ohm
R2 = 1 ohm
R3 = 1 ohm
R4 = 1 ohm

2.

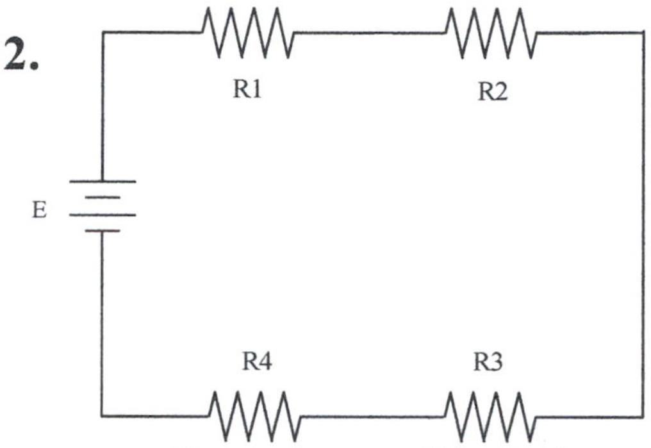
R1
R2
E
R4
R3

E = ______
I_T = 3 amperes
R1 = 0.5 ohms
R2 = 1 ohm
R3 = 0.5 ohms
R4 = 1 ohm

3.

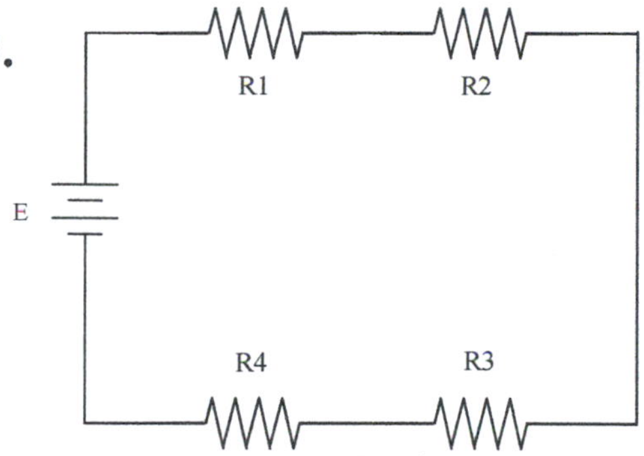
R1
R2
E
R4
R3

E = 4 volts
I_T = ______
R_T = 3 ohms

4.

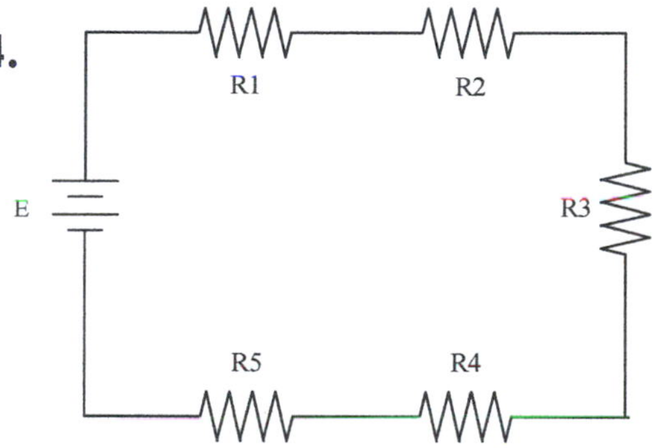
R1
R2
E
R3
R5
R4

E = 12 volts
I_T = 1 amperes
R1 = 2 ohm
R2 = ______
R3 = 4 ohms
R4 = 3 ohms
R5 = 1 ohm

5.

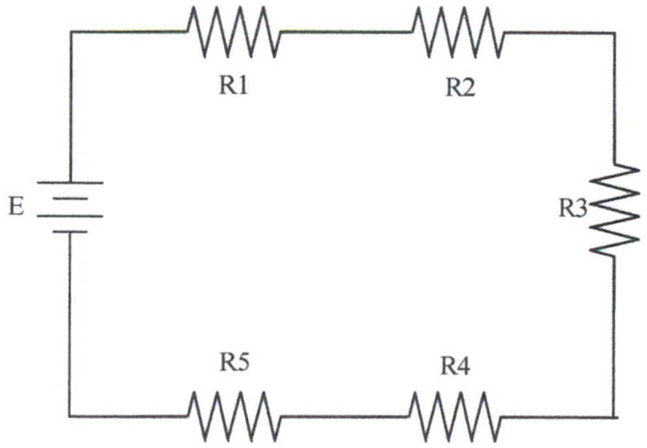
R1
R2
E
R3
R5
R4

E = 24 volts
I_T = 12 amperes
R1 = 0.5 ohms
R2 = 0.5 ohms
R3 = ______
R4 = 0.5 ohms
R5 = 0.25 ohms

6.

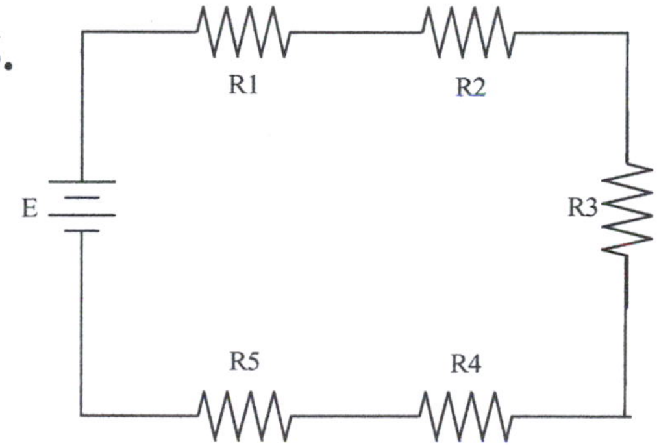
R1
R2
E
R3
R5
R4

E = 24 volts
I_T = 3 amperes
R1 = 2 ohms
R2 = 1 ohm
R3 = 2 ohms
R4 = ______
R5 = 2 ohms

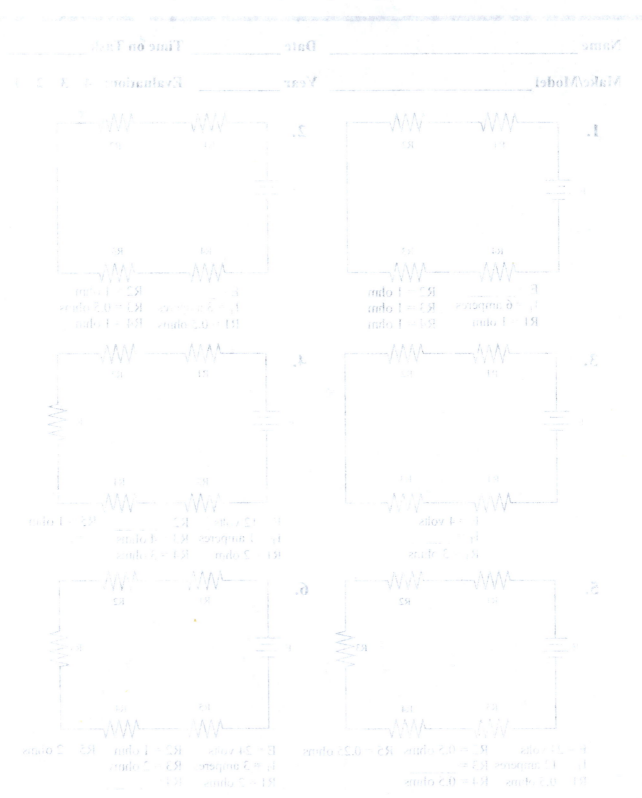

We Support NATEF

Parallel Circuit Worksheet #1

Meets NATEF Task: (A6-A-2) Diagnose Electrical/Electronic Integrity for Series, Parallel, and Series-Parallel Circuits Using Principles of Electricity (Ohm's Law).

Name ______________________ **Date** __________ **Time on Task** __________

Make/Model ______________________ **Year** __________ **Evaluation: 4 3 2 1**

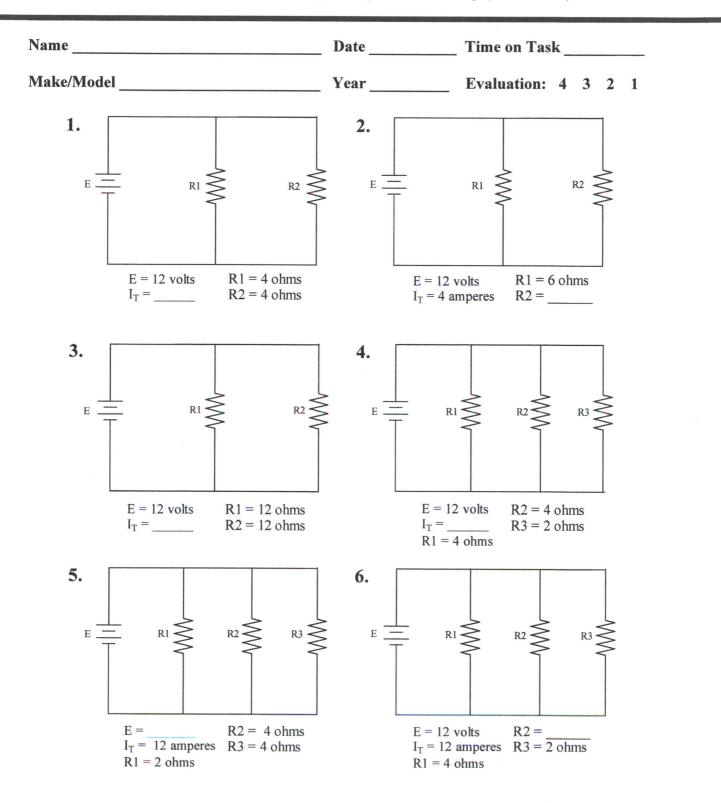

1.

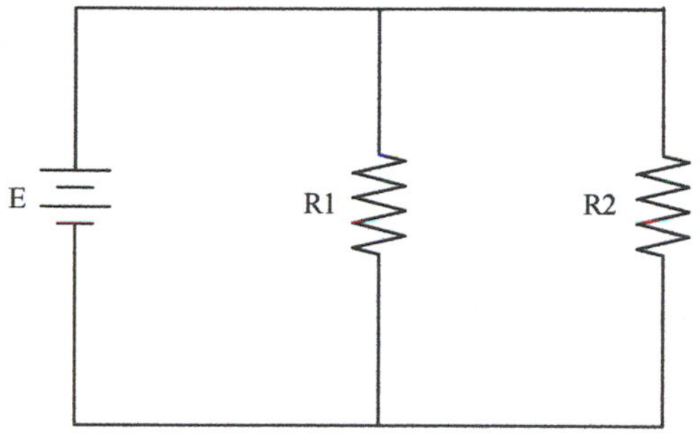
E
R1
R2

E = 12 volts
I_T = ______
R1 = 4 ohms
R2 = 4 ohms

2.

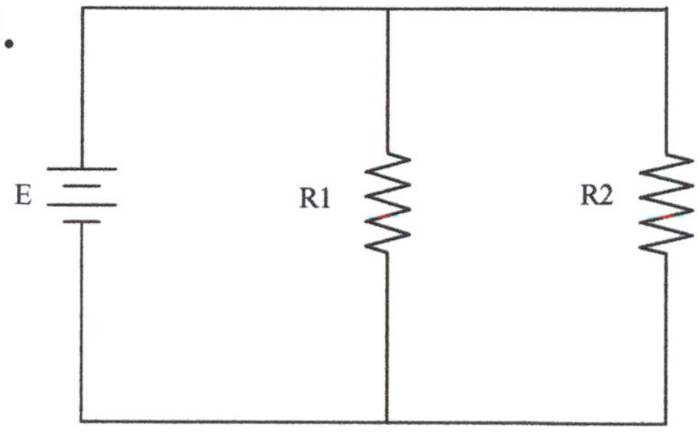
E
R1
R2

E = 12 volts
I_T = 4 amperes
R1 = 6 ohms
R2 = ______

3.

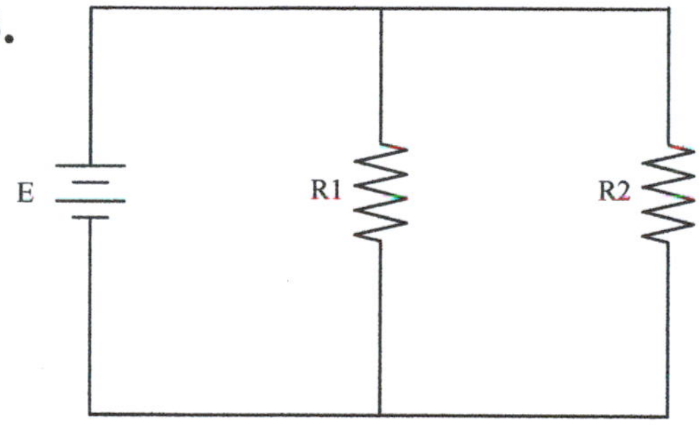
E
R1
R2

E = 12 volts
I_T = ______
R1 = 12 ohms
R2 = 12 ohms

4.

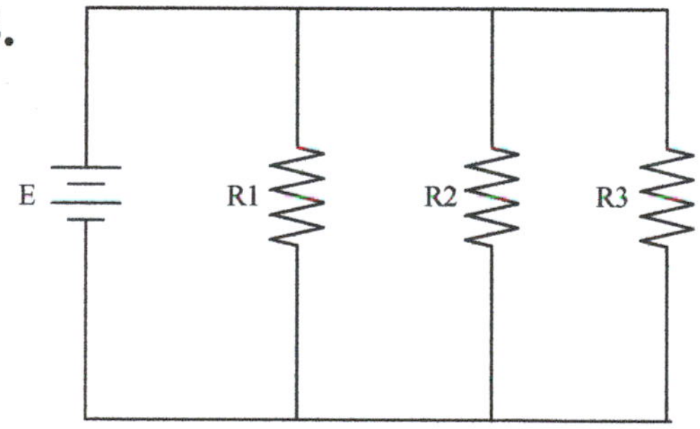
E
R1
R2
R3

E = 12 volts
I_T = ______
R1 = 4 ohms
R2 = 4 ohms
R3 = 2 ohms

5.

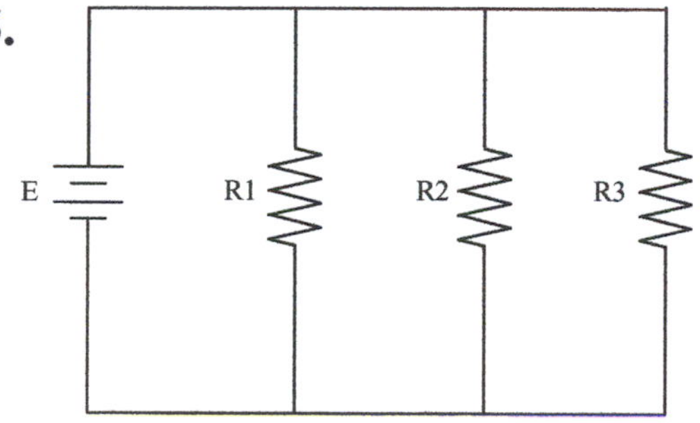
E
R1
R2
R3

E = ______
I_T = 12 amperes
R1 = 2 ohms
R2 = 4 ohms
R3 = 4 ohms

6.

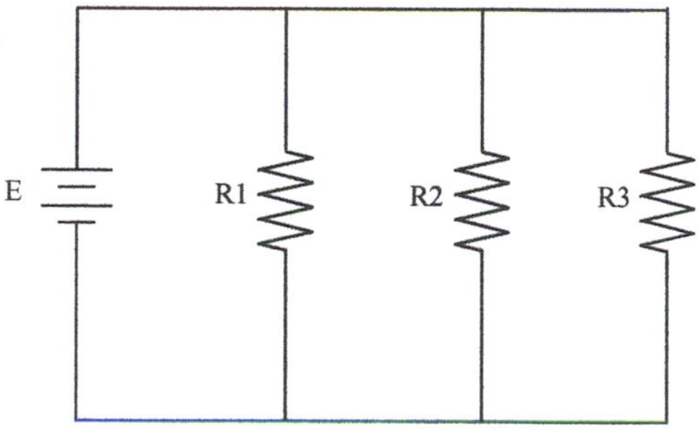
E
R1
R2
R3

E = 12 volts
I_T = 12 amperes
R1 = 4 ohms
R2 = ______
R3 = 2 ohms

Parallel Circuit Worksheet #2

Meets NATEF Task: (A6-A-2) Diagnose Electrical/Electronic Integrity for Series, Parallel, and Series-Parallel Circuits Using Principles of Electricity (Ohm's Law).

Name ____________________ **Date** __________ **Time on Task** __________

Make/Model ____________________ **Year** __________ **Evaluation: 4 3 2 1**

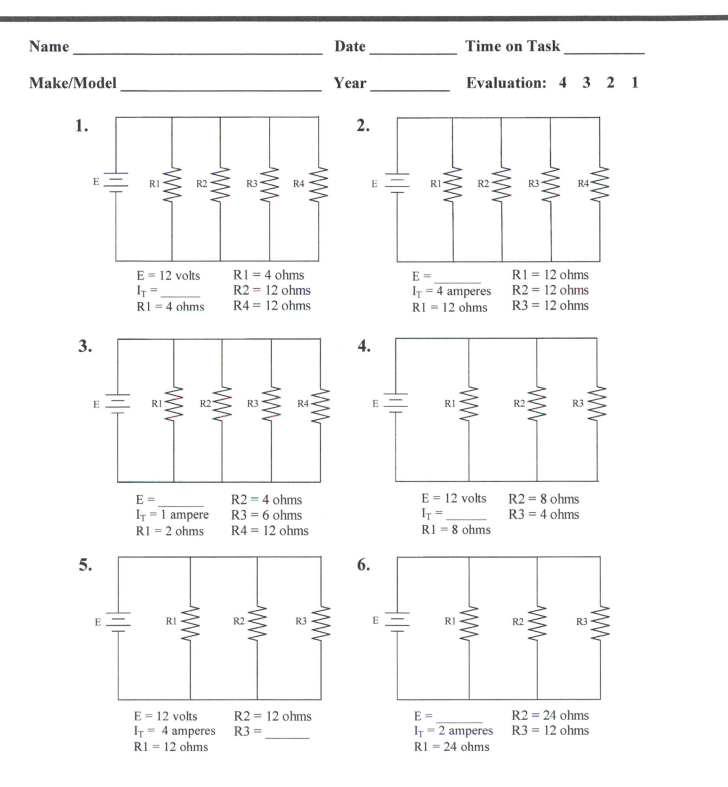

1.

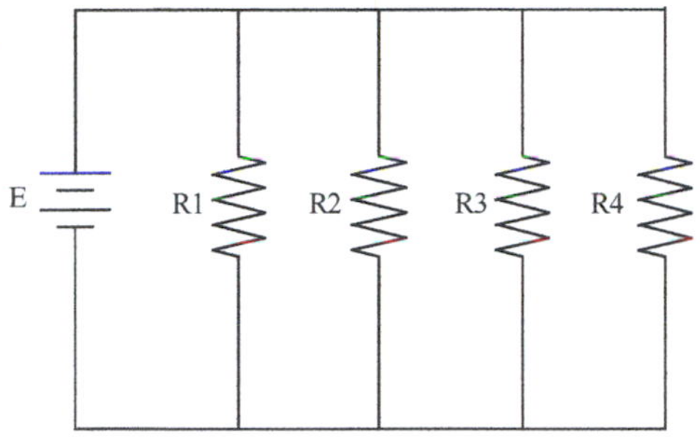
E
R1
R2
R3
R4

E = 12 volts
I_T = ______
R1 = 4 ohms
R1 = 4 ohms
R2 = 12 ohms
R4 = 12 ohms

2.

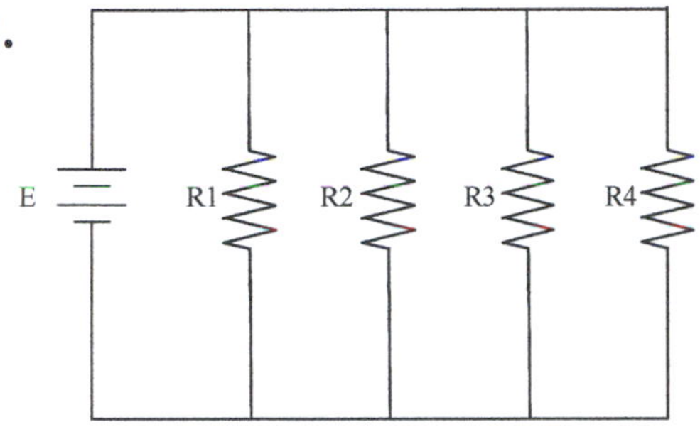
E
R1
R2
R3
R4

E = ______
I_T = 4 amperes
R1 = 12 ohms
R1 = 12 ohms
R2 = 12 ohms
R3 = 12 ohms

3.

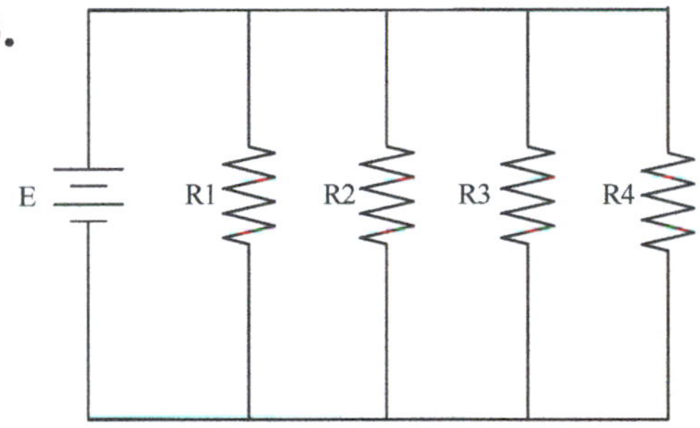
E
R1
R2
R3
R4

E = ______
I_T = 1 ampere
R1 = 2 ohms
R2 = 4 ohms
R3 = 6 ohms
R4 = 12 ohms

4.

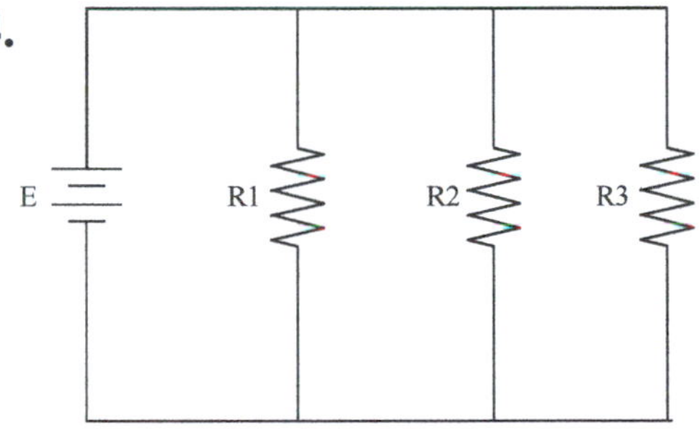
E
R1
R2
R3

E = 12 volts
I_T = ______
R1 = 8 ohms
R2 = 8 ohms
R3 = 4 ohms

5.

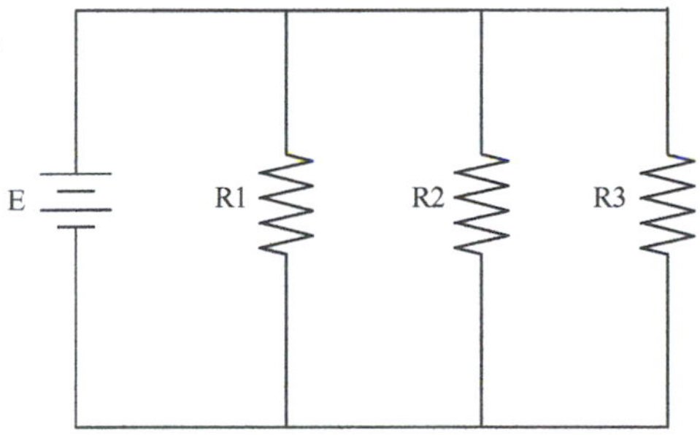
E
R1
R2
R3

E = 12 volts
I_T = 4 amperes
R1 = 12 ohms
R2 = 12 ohms
R3 = ______

6.

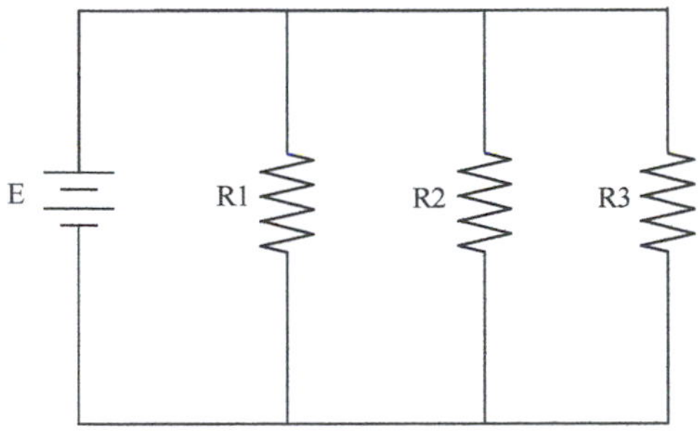
E
R1
R2
R3

E = ______
I_T = 2 amperes
R1 = 24 ohms
R2 = 24 ohms
R3 = 12 ohms

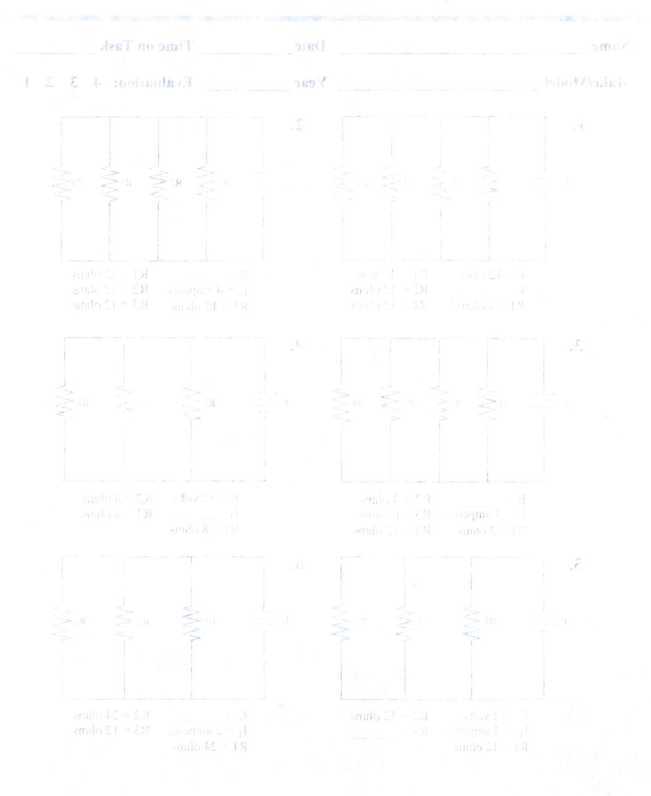

Parallel Circuit Worksheet #3

Meets NATEF Task: (A6-A-2) Diagnose Electrical/Electronic Integrity for Series, Parallel, and Series-Parallel Circuits Using Principles of Electricity (Ohm's Law).

Name ______________________ **Date** __________ **Time on Task** __________

Make/Model ______________________ **Year** __________ **Evaluation: 4 3 2 1**

1.

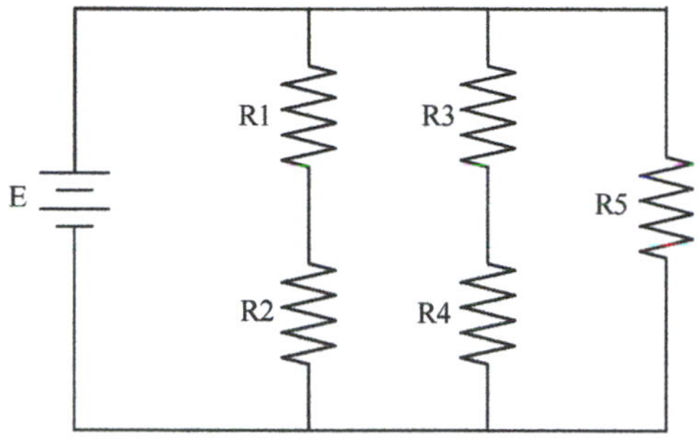
E
R1
R2
R3
R4
R5

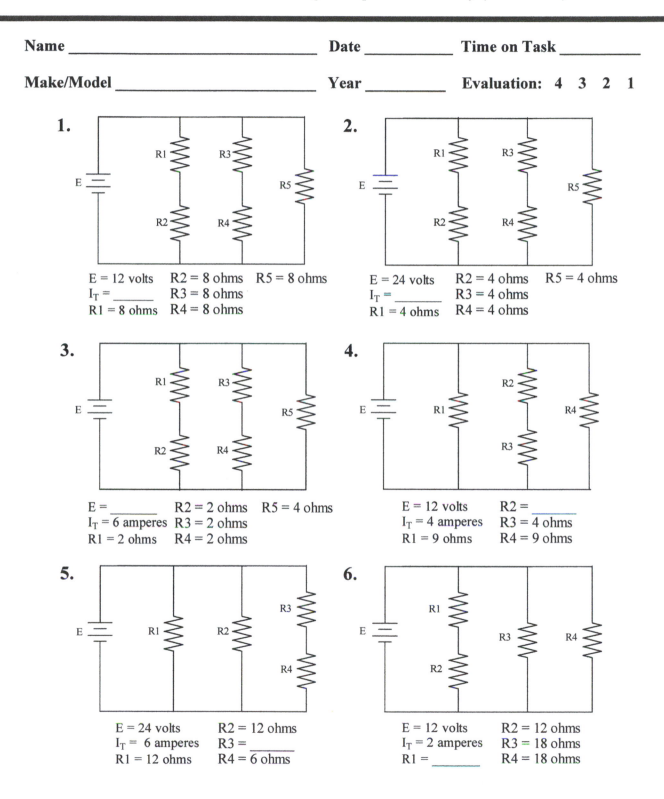

E = 12 volts R2 = 8 ohms R5 = 8 ohms
I_T = ______ R3 = 8 ohms
R1 = 8 ohms R4 = 8 ohms

2.

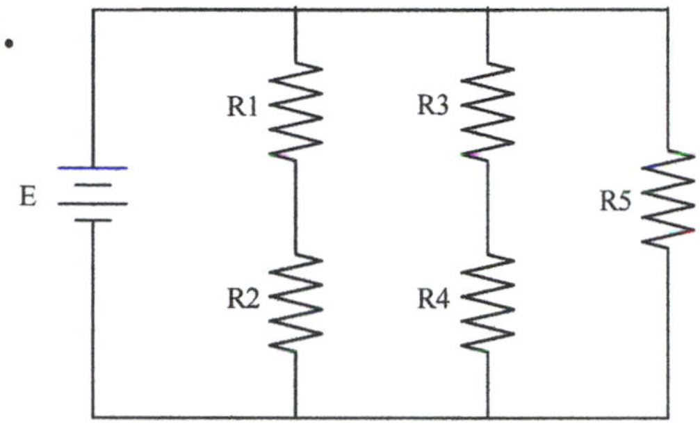
E
R1
R2
R3
R4
R5

E = 24 volts R2 = 4 ohms R5 = 4 ohms
I_T = ______ R3 = 4 ohms
R1 = 4 ohms R4 = 4 ohms

3.

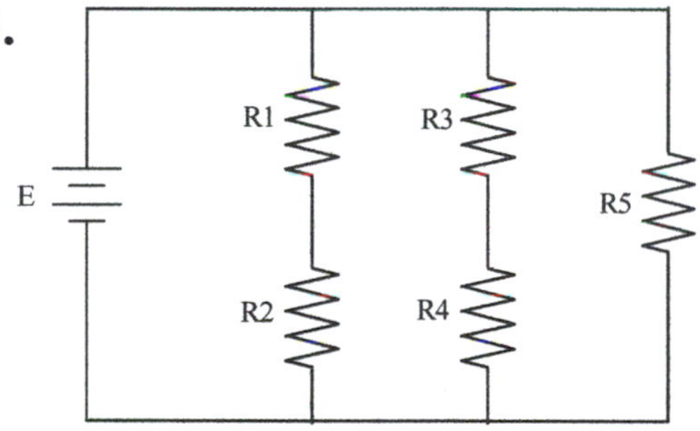
E
R1
R2
R3
R4
R5

E = ______ R2 = 2 ohms R5 = 4 ohms
I_T = 6 amperes R3 = 2 ohms
R1 = 2 ohms R4 = 2 ohms

4.

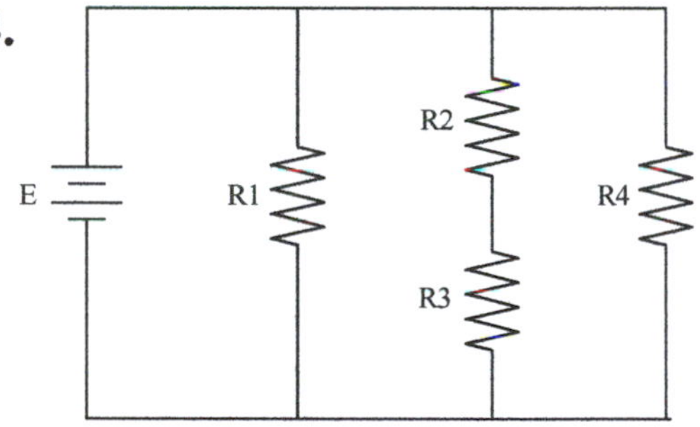
E
R1
R2
R3
R4

E = 12 volts R2 = ______
I_T = 4 amperes R3 = 4 ohms
R1 = 9 ohms R4 = 9 ohms

5.

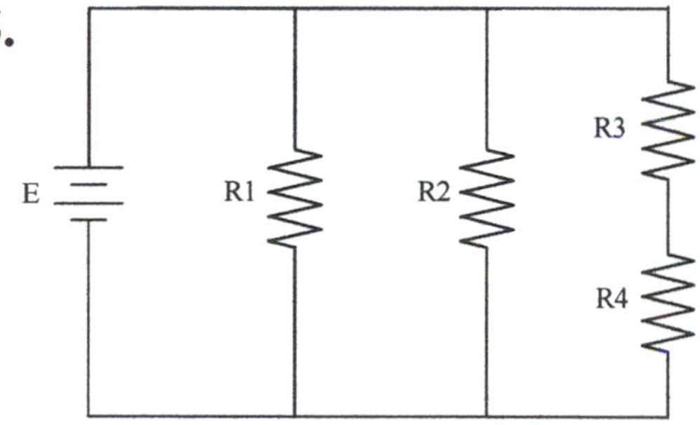
E
R1
R2
R3
R4

E = 24 volts R2 = 12 ohms
I_T = 6 amperes R3 = ______
R1 = 12 ohms R4 = 6 ohms

6.

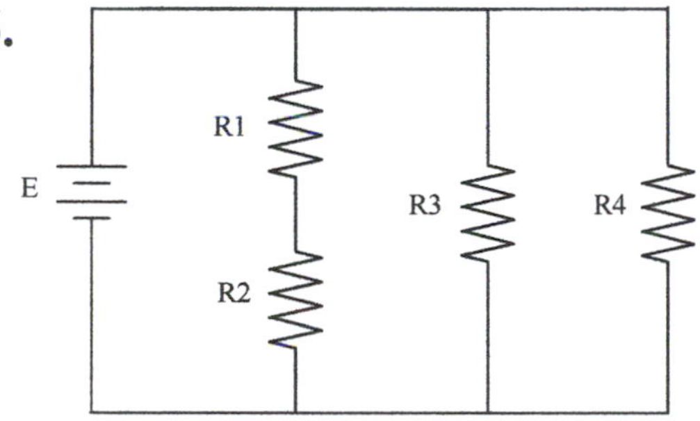
E
R1
R2
R3
R4

E = 12 volts R2 = 12 ohms
I_T = 2 amperes R3 = 18 ohms
R1 = ______ R4 = 18 ohms

We Support NATEF

Series-Parallel Circuit Worksheet #1

Meets NATEF Task: (A6-A-2) Diagnose Electrical/Electronic Integrity for Series, Parallel, and Series-Parallel Circuits Using Principles of Electricity (Ohm's Law).

Name ______________________ **Date** __________ **Time on Task** __________

Make/Model ______________________ **Year** __________ **Evaluation: 4 3 2 1**

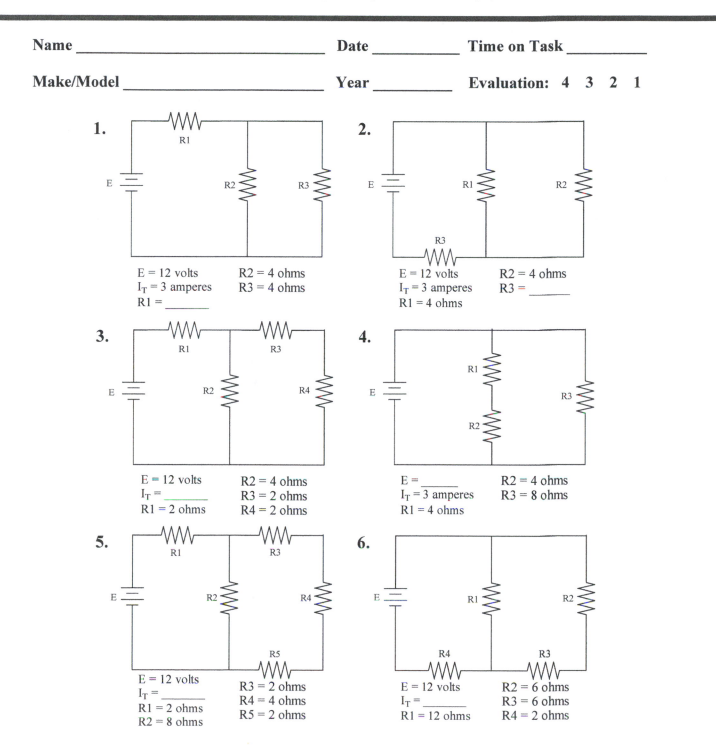

1.

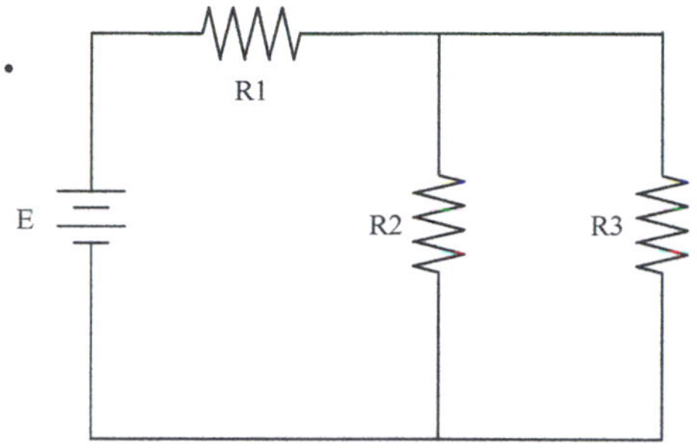
R1
E
R2
R3

E = 12 volts
I_T = 3 amperes
R1 = ______
R2 = 4 ohms
R3 = 4 ohms

2.

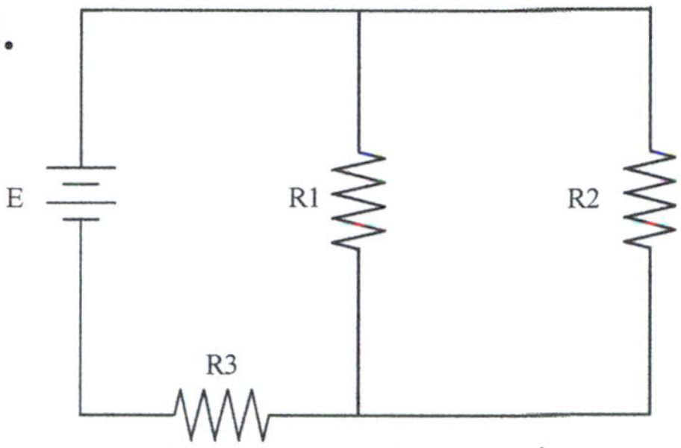
E
R1
R2
R3

E = 12 volts
I_T = 3 amperes
R1 = 4 ohms
R2 = 4 ohms
R3 = ______

3.

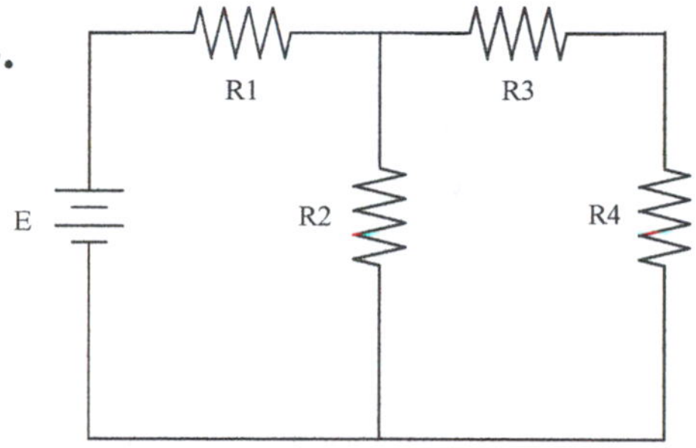
R1
R3
E
R2
R4

E = 12 volts
I_T = ______
R1 = 2 ohms
R2 = 4 ohms
R3 = 2 ohms
R4 = 2 ohms

4.

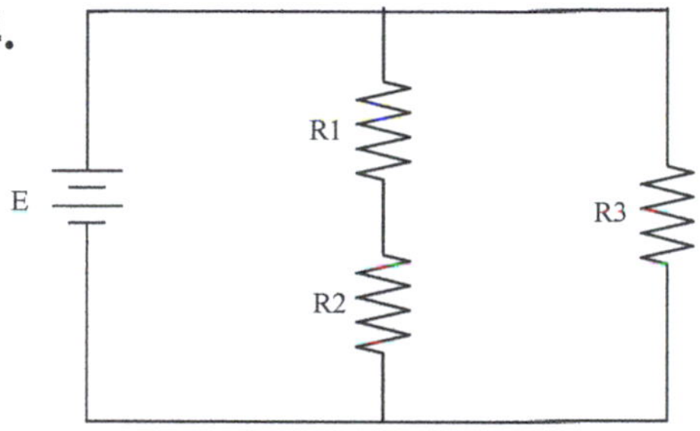
R1
E
R3
R2

E = ______
I_T = 3 amperes
R1 = 4 ohms
R2 = 4 ohms
R3 = 8 ohms

5.

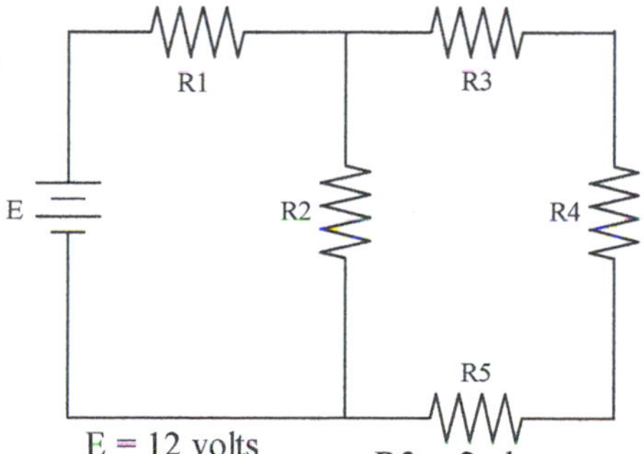
R1
R3
E
R2
R4
R5

E = 12 volts
I_T = ______
R1 = 2 ohms
R2 = 8 ohms
R3 = 2 ohms
R4 = 4 ohms
R5 = 2 ohms

6.

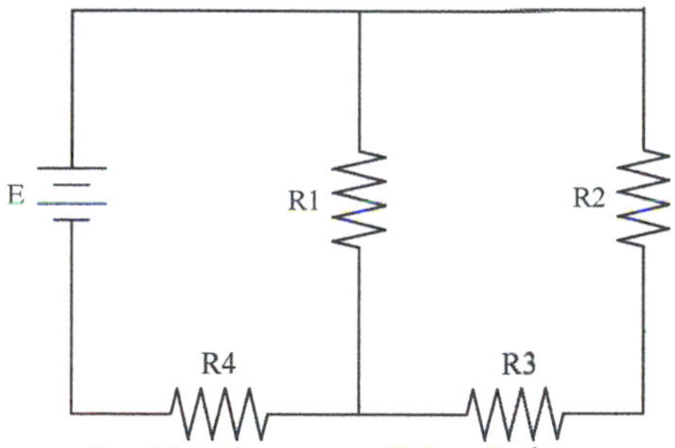
E
R1
R2
R4
R3

E = 12 volts
I_T = ______
R1 = 12 ohms
R2 = 6 ohms
R3 = 6 ohms
R4 = 2 ohms

Series-Parallel Circuit Worksheet #2

Meets NATEF Task: (A6-A-2) Diagnose Electrical/Electronic Integrity for Series, Parallel, and Series-Parallel Circuits Using Principles of Electricity (Ohm's Law).

Name ______________________ **Date** __________ **Time on Task** __________

Make/Model ______________________ **Year** __________ **Evaluation:** 4 3 2 1

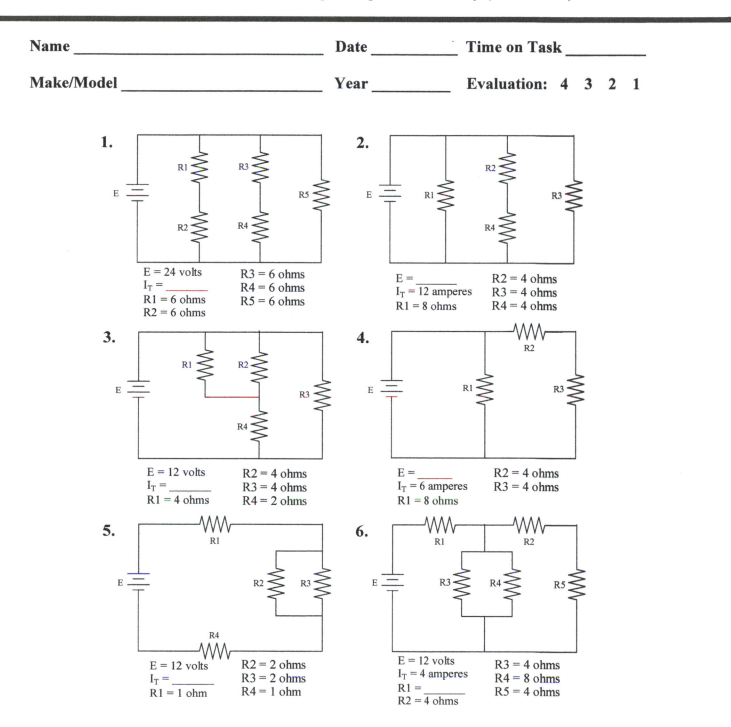

1.

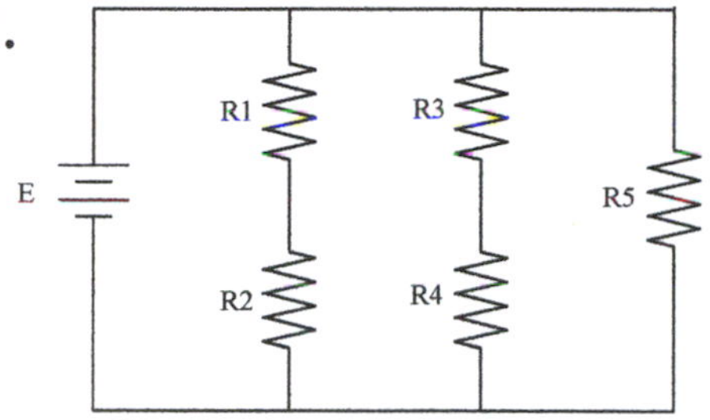
E
R1
R2
R3
R4
R5

E = 24 volts
I_T = ______
R1 = 6 ohms
R2 = 6 ohms
R3 = 6 ohms
R4 = 6 ohms
R5 = 6 ohms

2.

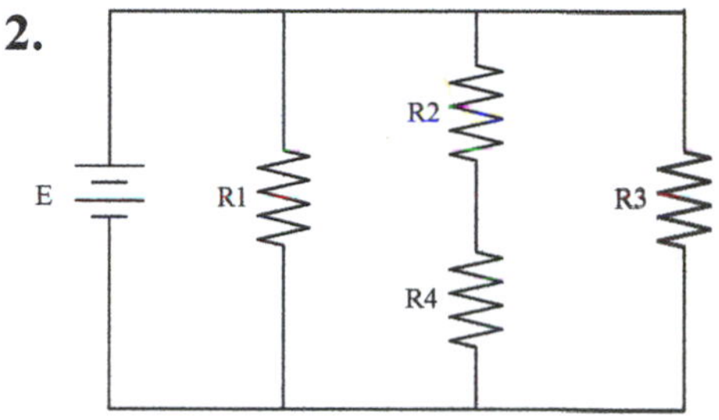
E
R1
R2
R4
R3

E = ______
I_T = 12 amperes
R1 = 8 ohms
R2 = 4 ohms
R3 = 4 ohms
R4 = 4 ohms

3.

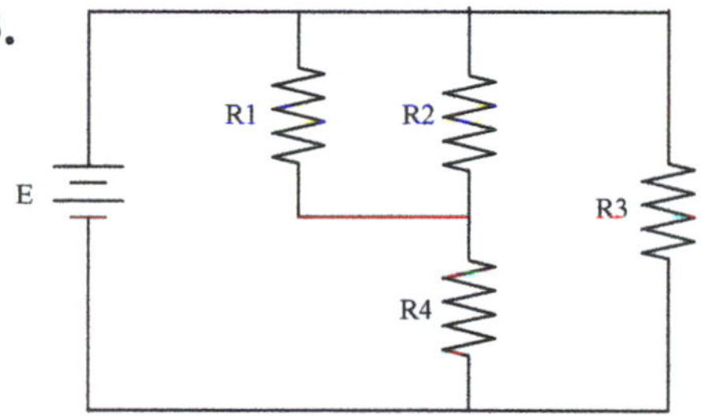
E
R1
R2
R4
R3

E = 12 volts
I_T = ______
R1 = 4 ohms
R2 = 4 ohms
R3 = 4 ohms
R4 = 2 ohms

4.

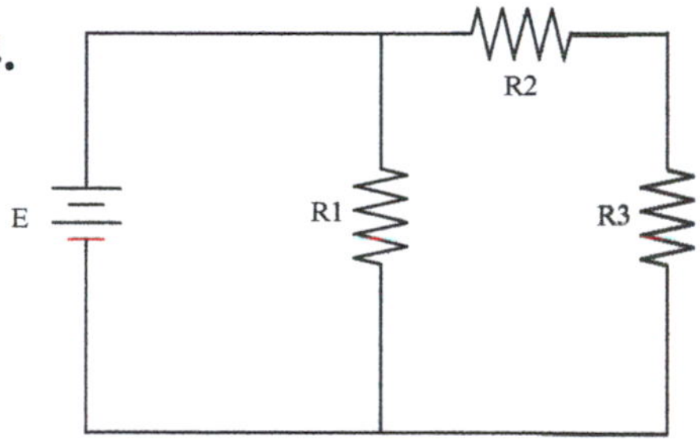
E
R2
R1
R3

E = ______
I_T = 6 amperes
R1 = 8 ohms
R2 = 4 ohms
R3 = 4 ohms

5.

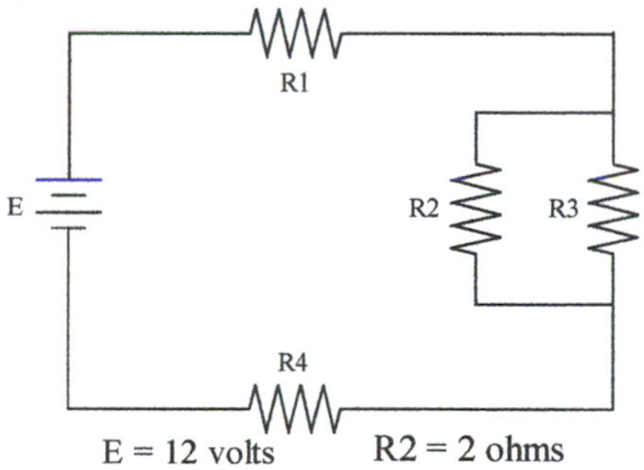
R1
E
R2
R3
R4

E = 12 volts
I_T = ______
R1 = 1 ohm
R2 = 2 ohms
R3 = 2 ohms
R4 = 1 ohm

6.

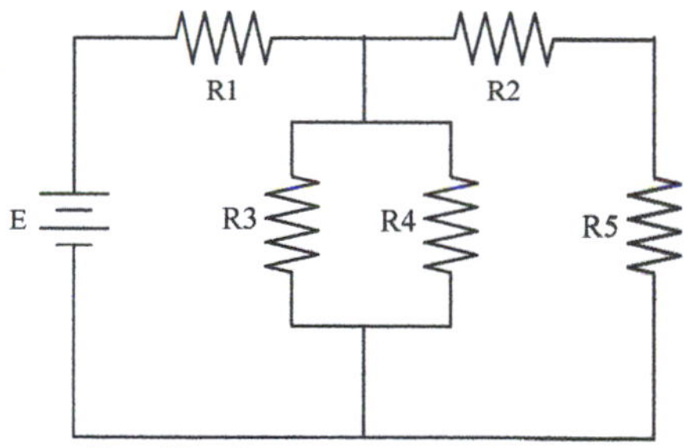
R1
R2
E
R3
R4
R5

E = 12 volts
I_T = 4 amperes
R1 = ______
R2 = 4 ohms
R3 = 4 ohms
R4 = 8 ohms
R5 = 4 ohms

We Support NATEF

Series-Parallel Circuit Worksheet #3

Meets NATEF Task: (A6-A-2) Diagnose Electrical/Electronic Integrity for Series, Parallel, and Series-Parallel Circuits Using Principles of Electricity (Ohm's Law).

Name ______________________________ **Date** __________ **Time on Task** __________

Make/Model ________________________ **Year** _________ **Evaluation: 4 3 2 1**

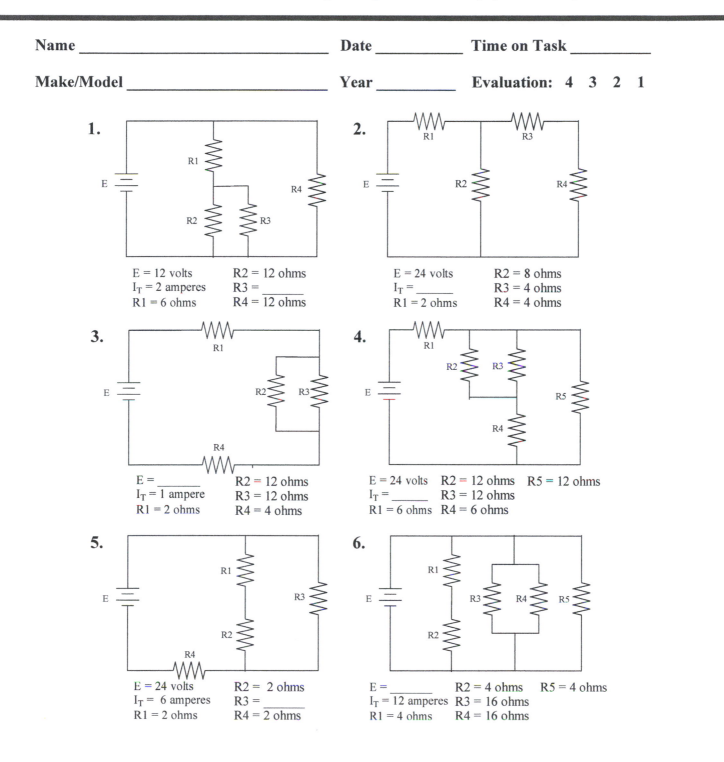

1.

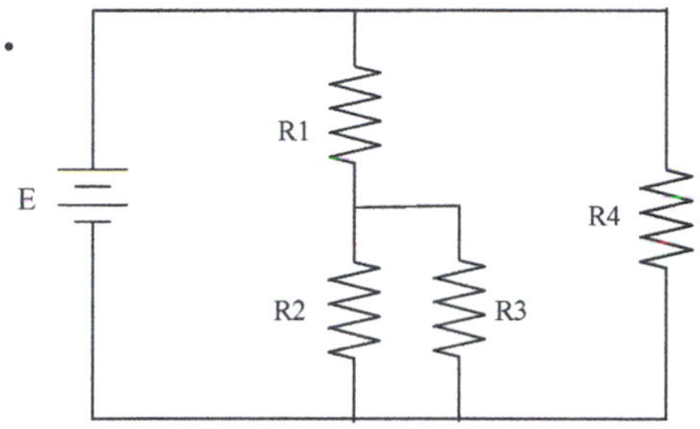
E
R1
R2
R3
R4

E = 12 volts
I_T = 2 amperes
R1 = 6 ohms
R2 = 12 ohms
R3 = ______
R4 = 12 ohms

2.

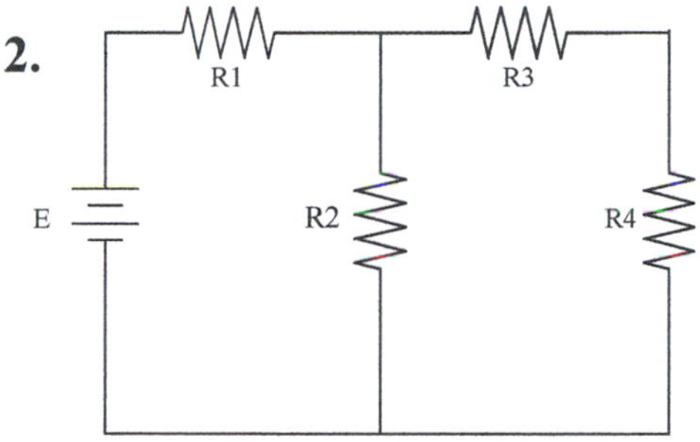
R1
R3
E
R2
R4

E = 24 volts
I_T = ______
R1 = 2 ohms
R2 = 8 ohms
R3 = 4 ohms
R4 = 4 ohms

3.

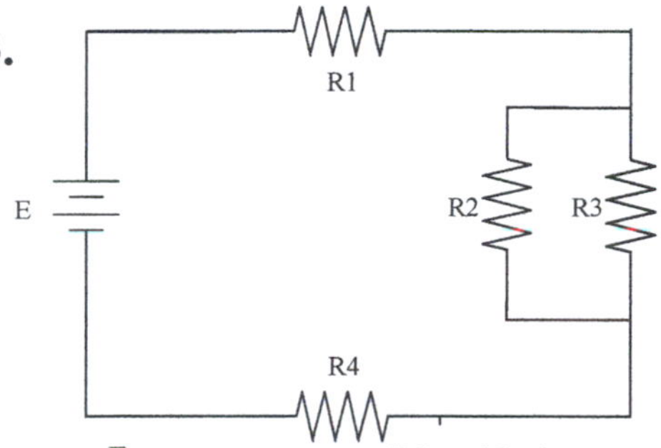
R1
E
R2
R3
R4

E = ______
I_T = 1 ampere
R1 = 2 ohms
R2 = 12 ohms
R3 = 12 ohms
R4 = 4 ohms

4.

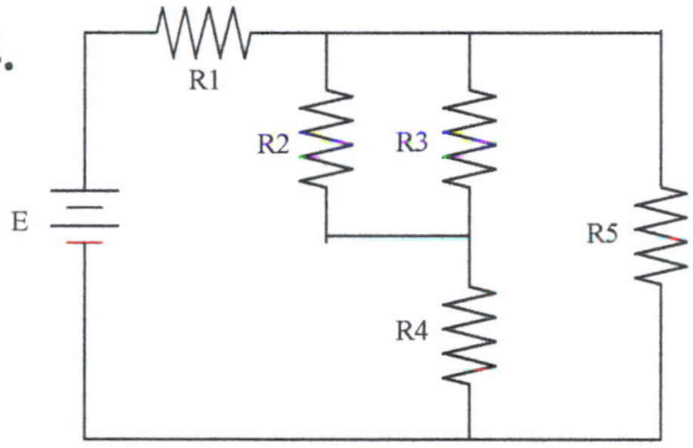
R1
R2
R3
E
R5
R4

E = 24 volts
I_T = ______
R1 = 6 ohms
R2 = 12 ohms
R3 = 12 ohms
R4 = 6 ohms
R5 = 12 ohms

5.

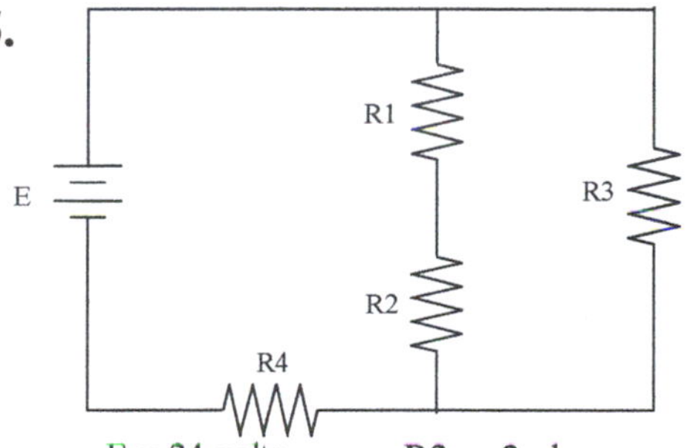
R1
E
R3
R2
R4

E = 24 volts
I_T = 6 amperes
R1 = 2 ohms
R2 = 2 ohms
R3 = ______
R4 = 2 ohms

6.

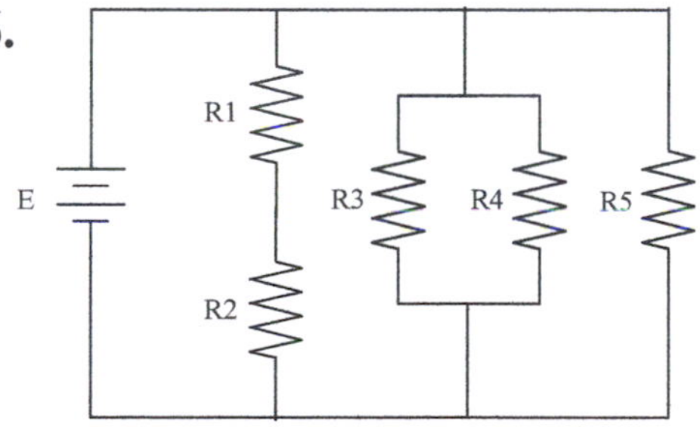
R1
E
R3
R4
R5
R2

E = ______
I_T = 12 amperes
R1 = 4 ohms
R2 = 4 ohms
R3 = 16 ohms
R4 = 16 ohms
R5 = 4 ohms

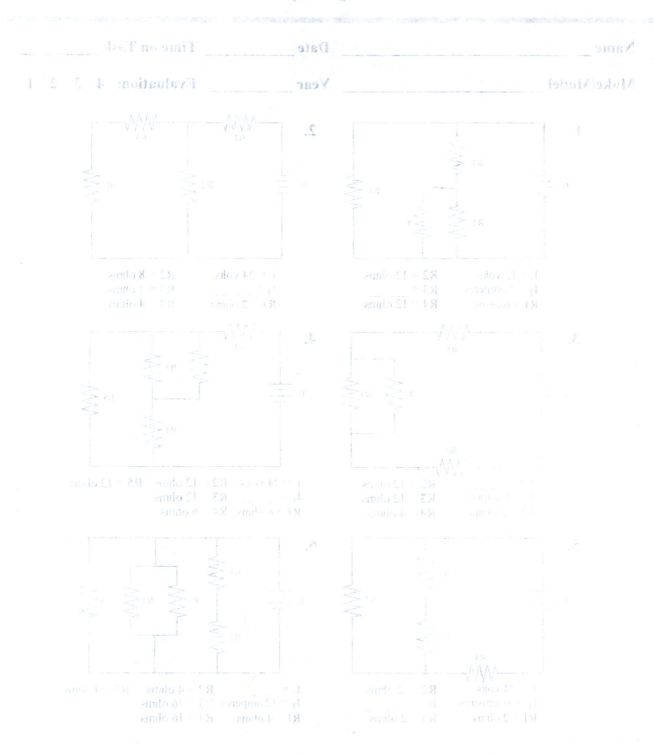

Digital Multimeter Use for Electrical Problems

Meets NATEF Task: (A6-A-3) Demonstrate the proper use of a digital multimeter (DMM) during diagnosis of electrical circuit problems. (P-1)

Name ______________________ **Date** __________ **Time on Task** __________

Make/Model ______________________ **Year** __________ **Evaluation: 4 3 2 1**

_____ **1.** Check service information on the correct procedure for checking charging system voltage.

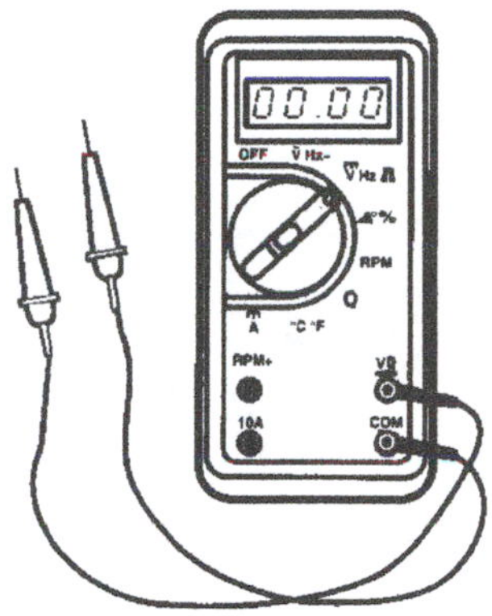

____

____

a. Which position on the digital multimeter should be selected to check charging system voltage?

____

What is the specified voltage? _________

What is the actual voltage? _________

b. Which position should selected to check the voltage drop of the charging system? __________________

What is the specified voltage drop? _________

What is the actual voltage drop? _________

_____ **2.** Check service information regarding the specified resistance for spark plug wires.

____

Which position on the DMM should be selected to measure spark plug wire resistance? __________________

What is the specified resistance? ___________

What is the actual (measured) resistance? ___________

_____ **3.** Check service information regarding the specified battery drain test (parasitic draw) test procedures.

____

Which position on the DMM should be selected to measure battery electrical drain? __________________

What is the specified maximum battery electrical drain? __________

What is the actual (measured) battery electrical drain? ___________

Test Light Usage

Meets NATEF Task: (A6-A-5) Check electrical circuits with a test light; determine the necessary action. (P-2)

Name ______________________ **Date** __________ **Time on Task** __________

Make/Model ______________________ **Year** __________ **Evaluation: 4 3 2 1**

_____ **1.** Check service information regarding which wire color(s) is the brake light and which is the tail light. Using a test light, check for voltage to the brake lights and tail lights at the rear of the vehicle.

____

____

a. Brake light: ____ **OK** ____ **NOT OK** (describe fault) ______________

____

b. Tail light: ____ **OK** ____ **NOT OK** (describe fault) ______________

____

_____ **2.** Using a test light, check all of the fuses in the vehicle.

NOTE: The ignition switch and/or lights need to be on to supply power to some fuses.

List all good fuses: ______________________________

____

_____ **3.** Based on the above activities, what is the necessary action? ______________

____

____

____

____

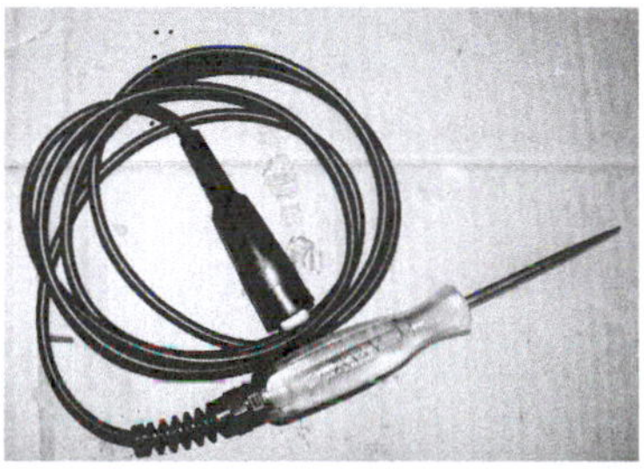

Circuit Testing Using a Fused Jumper Wire

Meets NATEF Task: (A6-A-6) Check electrical circuits using fused jumper wire; determine the necessary action. (P-2)

Name ______________________ **Date** __________ **Time on Task** __________

Make/Model ______________________ **Year** __________ **Evaluation: 4 3 2 1**

CAUTION: A fused jumper wire should never be used to bypass an electrical load device. A fused jumper wire should only be used to bypass circuit control devices such as switches or relays.

_____ **1.** Check service information for a diagnostic test procedure that includes the use of a fused jumper wire.

____

____

____

_____ **2.** A horn circuit is a commonly used circuit to show the use of a fused jumper wire.

a. Locate the horn (describe the location):

____

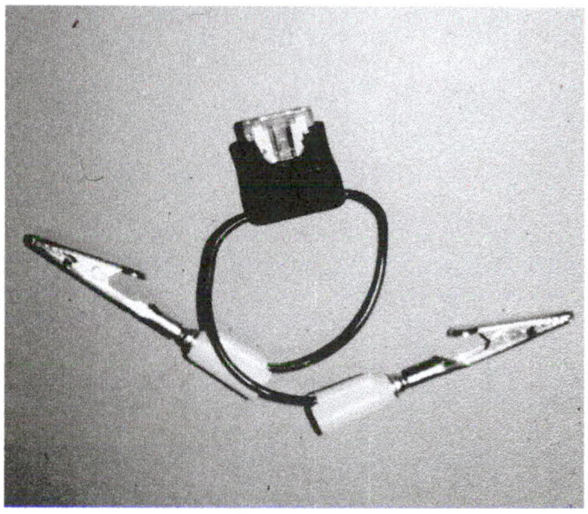

b. Disconnect the wire from the horn.

c. Connect one end of the fused jumper wire to the terminal of the horn.

d. Touch the other end of the fused jumper wire to the positive (+) terminal of the battery.

e. The horn should work. **OK** ____ **NOT OK** ____

_____ **3.** Based on the test results, what is the necessary action? ______________________

____

Oscilloscope

Meets NATEF Task: (A6-A-14) Diagnose electrical and electronic concerns using an oscilloscope; determine the necessary action. (P-1)

Name ______________________ **Date** __________ **Time on Task** __________

Make/Model ______________________ **Year** __________ **Evaluation: 4 3 2 1**

_____ **1.** Check service information for the recommended usage of an oscilloscope to diagnose electrical or electronic concerns. Describe the tests recommended. ______________

____

____

_____ **2.** According to service information, which system can/should be tested using an oscilloscope? (Check all that apply.)

____ Wheel speed sensor

____ Crankshaft position sensor

____ Camshaft position sensor

____ Secondary ignition

____ Serial data communication circuits

____ Audio circuits

____ Other (describe) ______________

____

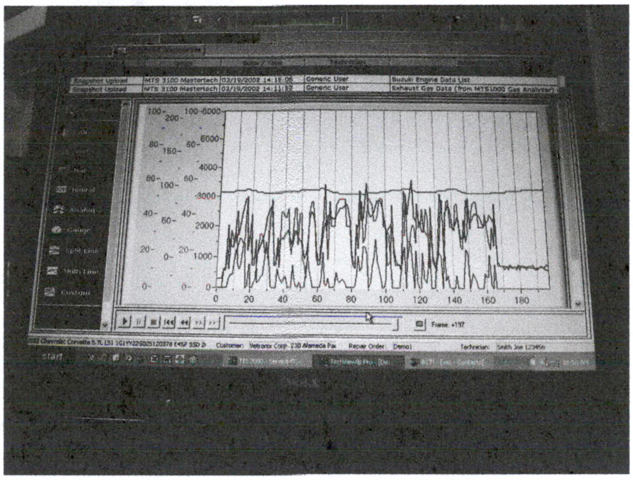
0 20 40 60 80 100 120 140 160 180

_____ **3.** Which system(s) was tested using an oscilloscope? ______________________

____

____

_____ **4.** Based on the test results, what is the necessary action? ______________________

____

____

____

Fusible Links, Circuit Breakers, and Fuses

Meets NATEF Task: (A6-A-9) Inspect and test fusible links, circuit breakers, and fuses; determine the necessary action. (P-1)

Name ______________________ **Date** __________ **Time on Task** __________

Make/Model ______________________ **Year** __________ **Evaluation: 4 3 2 1**

_____ **1.** Check service information for the location procedures for all of the fusible links, circuit breakers, and fuses.

A. Fusible links: Number __________ Location ______________

B. Circuit breakers Number __________ Location ______________

C. Fuses Number __________ Location ______________

_____ **2.** Describe the specified testing procedures.

A. Fusible links ________________________________

B. Circuit breakers ________________________________

C. Fuses ________________________________

NOTE: Many circuit breakers and fuses are not powered until the ignition switch is turned to the on (run) position or until the lights are turned on.

_____ **3.** Test the circuit protection devices.

A. Fusible links **OK** ____ **NOT OK** ____ (which ones?) __________

B. Circuit breakers **OK** ____ **NOT OK** ____ (which ones?) __________

C. Fuses **OK** ____ **NOT OK** ____ (which ones?) __________

_____ **4.** Based on the tests, what is the necessary action?

____

____

____

We Support NATEF

Inspect and Test the Switches

Meets NATEF Task: (A6-A-10) Inspect and test switches, connectors, relays, and wires; determine the necessary action. (P-1)

Name ______________________ **Date** __________ **Time on Task** __________

Make/Model ______________________ **Year** __________ **Evaluation: 4 3 2 1**

_____ **1.** Check service information for the specified procedures for inspecting and testing switches.

____

____

_____ **2.** Check everything that does and does not work by operating all switches in the vehicle. List any and all circuits that do not function correctly when the switch is moved.

_______________ _______________ _______________

_______________ _______________ _______________

_____ **3.** Are any switch inputs to the body computer or module? If so, list those that can be monitored using a scan tool.

Switch Inputs to Computer/Module	**Operation Viewable on Scan Tool?**

_____ **4.** Test a relay.

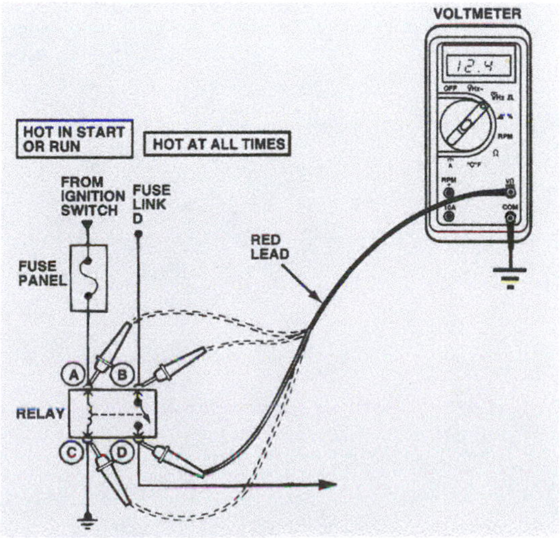
VOLTMETER
12.4
HOT IN START OR RUN
HOT AT ALL TIMES
FROM IGNITION SWITCH
FUSE LINK D
FUSE PANEL
RED LEAD
RELAY
A
B
C
D

_____ **5.** Based on the inspection and testing procedures, what is the necessary action?

____

____

Inspect Wiring and Connectors

Meets NATEF Task: (A6-A-11) Inspect and test switches, connectors, relays, and wires; determine the necessary action. (P-1)

Name ______________________ **Date** __________ **Time on Task** __________

Make/Model ______________________ **Year** __________ **Evaluation: 4 3 2 1**

_____ **1.** Check service information for the specified procedures for inspecting and testing wires and connectors.

____

____

_____ **2.** Most service information recommends that all wiring and connectors be inspected visually, especially where wiring is routed near sources of heat or where wiring is subject to movement. Perform a thorough visual inspection of all wires and connectors and note any faults.

Wire or Connector Fault(s)	Location (describe)
______________________	______________________
______________________	______________________
______________________	______________________
______________________	______________________

_____ **3.** Perform a voltage drop test of the cables or wires. Voltage should measure less than 0.2 volt drop.

_____ **4.** Based on your inspection and testing, what is the necessary action?

____

____

____

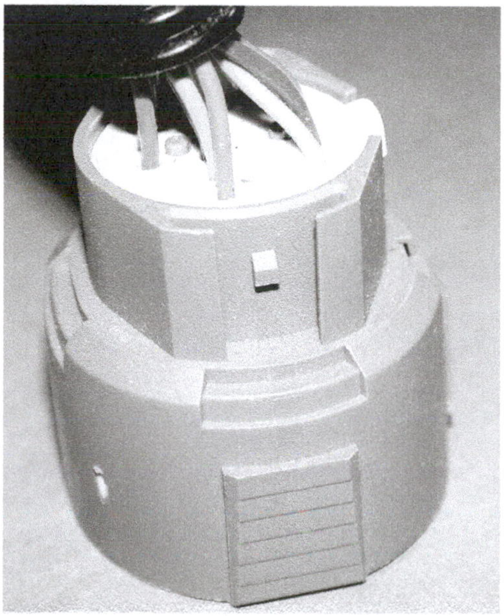

We Support NATEF

Wire Harness and Connector Repair

Meets NATEF Task: (A6-A-12) Repair wiring harnesses and connectors (P-1)

Name ______________________ **Date** __________ **Time on Task** __________

Make/Model ______________________ **Year** __________ **Evaluation:** 4 3 2 1

_____ **1.** Check service information for the specified procedures for repairing wiring harnesses and connectors. Describe:

____

____

_____ **2.** Perform a visual inspection and determine the following information regarding the wiring harnesses in the vehicle.

a. Is the wiring harness covered with corrugated plastic conduit?
_____ **Yes** _____ **No** (If no, disregard "B".)

b. Does the plastic corrugated conduit have a green or gray painted stripe?
_____ **Yes** _____ **No**

NOTE: The green or gray painted stripe indicates that the conduit is designed to withstand high temperatures up to about 300°F (150°C).

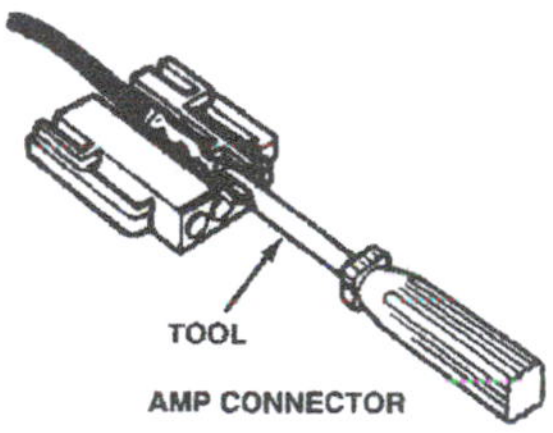
TOOL
AMP CONNECTOR

c. Is the wiring harness routed near any of these items?
_____ A heat source such as an EGR valve?
_____ **Yes** _____ **No**
_____ Close to moving components?
_____ **Yes** _____ **No**

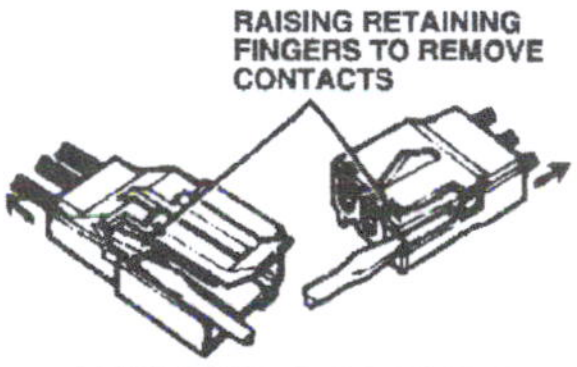
RAISING RETAINING FINGERS TO REMOVE CONTACTS
LOCKING WEDGE CONNECTOR

_____ **3.** Are the electrical connectors weather-proof?
_____ **Yes** _____ **No**

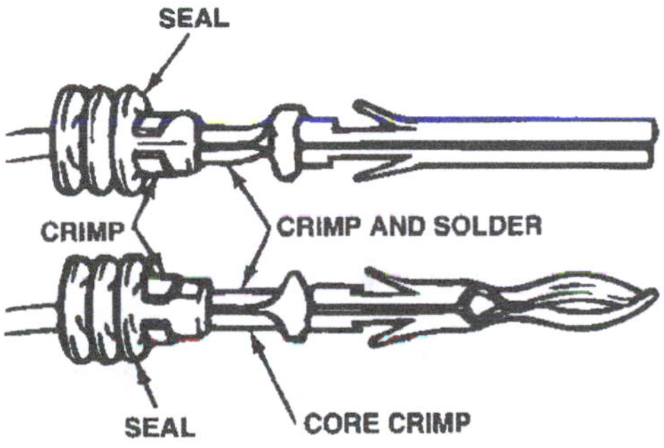
SEAL
CRIMP
CRIMP AND SOLDER
SEAL
CORE CRIMP

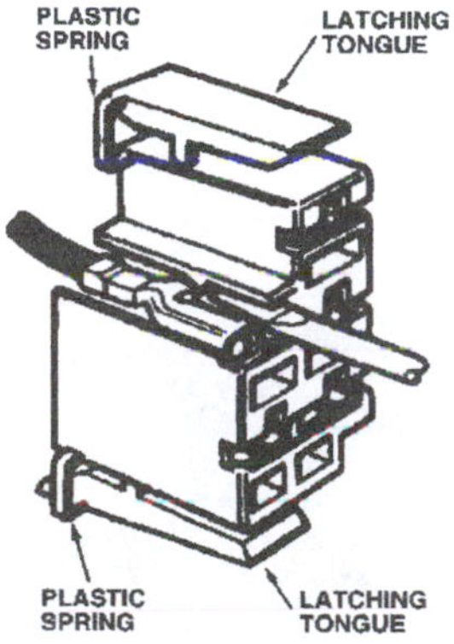
PLASTIC SPRING
LATCHING TONGUE
PLASTIC SPRING
LATCHING TONGUE
TANG CONNECTOR

Solder Wire Repair

Meets NATEF Task: (A6-A-13) Perform solder repair of electrical wiring. (P-1)

Name ______________________ **Date** __________ **Time on Task** __________

Make/Model ______________________ **Year** __________ **Evaluation: 4 3 2 1**

_____ **1.** Check service information for the specified procedures to follow when performing a solder wire repair.

____

____

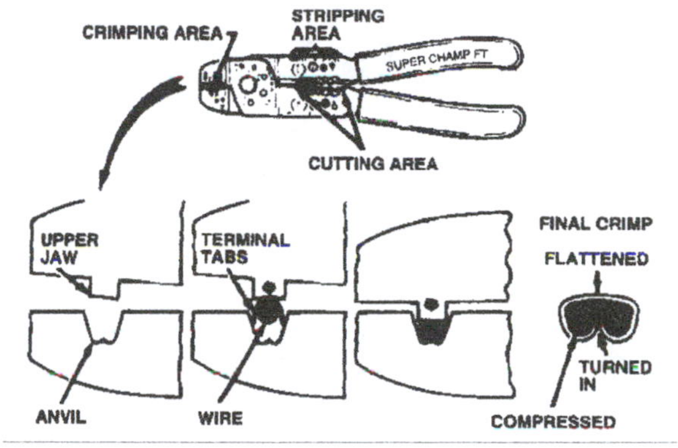
CRIMPING AREA
STRIPPING AREA
SUPER CHAMP FT
CUTTING AREA
UPPER JAW
TERMINAL TABS
FINAL CRIMP
FLATTENED
TURNED IN
ANVIL
WIRE
COMPRESSED

_____ **2.** Does the vehicle manufacturer specify that all hand-crimped terminals be soldered?

____ **Yes** ____ **No**

_____ **3.** Does the vehicle manufacturer specify the use of wire clips when soldering two wires together?

____ **Yes** ____ **No**

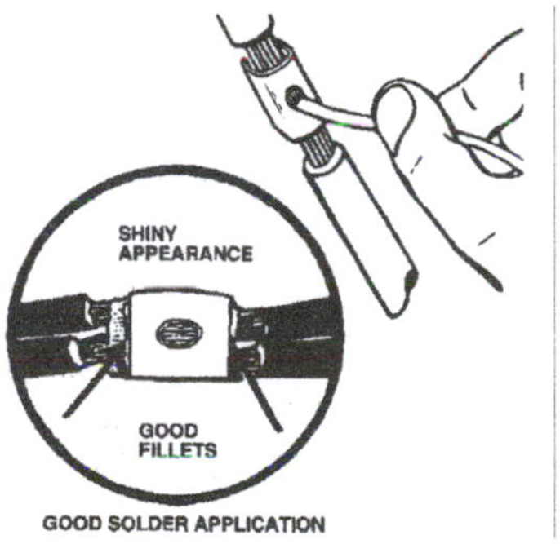
SHINY APPEARANCE
GOOD FILLETS
GOOD SOLDER APPLICATION

_____ **4.** Check all that apply:

____ Wire repair is to be covered with splice tape.
____ Wire repair is to be covered with heat-shrink tubing.
____ Wire repair is to be covered with adhesive-lined heat shrink tubing.
____ Other (describe) ______________________________

Identify/Interpret Electrical Systems Concerns

Meets NATEF Task: (A6-A-2) Identify and interpret electrical/electronic concerns; determine necessary action. (P-1)

Name ______________________ **Date** __________ **Time on Task** __________

Make/Model ______________________ **Year** __________ **Evaluation: 4 3 2 1**

_____ **1.** Describe electrical/electronic concerns. ______________________

____

_____ **2.** Can the concern be verified? ____ **Yes** ____ **No**

If no, ask the customer for additional information. ______________________

____

_____ **3.** Are there any stored diagnostic trouble codes (DTCs)?

____ **Yes** (describe) ______________________

____ **No**

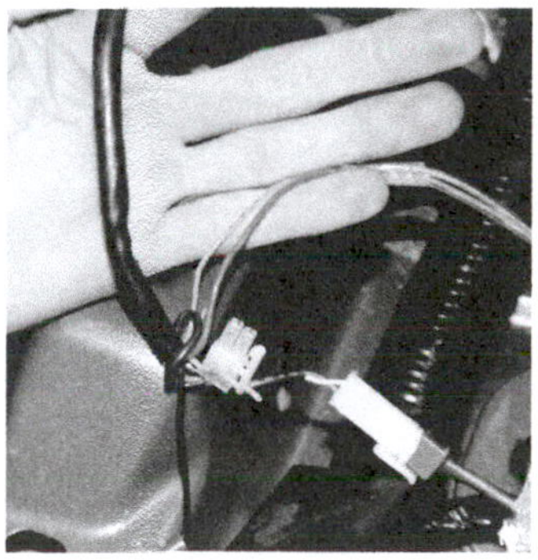

_____ **4.** Perform a thorough visual inspection of the related components and wiring.

____ **OK**

____ **NOT OK** (describe) ______________________

_____ **5.** Check service information for steps and procedures to determine and correct the fault.

____

____

_____ **6.** Based on the above inspection and research, what is the necessary action?

____

____

We Support NATEF

Diagnose Electrical/Electronic Circuits

Meets NATEF Task: (A6-A-7) Diagnose electrical/electronic integrity for series, parallel, and series-parallel circuits using principles of electricity (Ohm's Law). (P-1)

Name ______________________ **Date** __________ **Time on Task** __________

Make/Model ______________________ **Year** __________ **Evaluation: 4 3 2 1**

_____ **1.** Check service information to determine the specified diagnosis procedures to follow for a slowly operating wiper motor. This circuit is a:

____ Series

____ Parallel

____ Series-Parallel

_____ **2.** One tail light is dim, all other exterior lighting operates normally. Check service information to determine the specified diagnostic procedure to follow for a dim tail light.

This circuit is a:

____ Series

____ Parallel

____ Series-Parallel

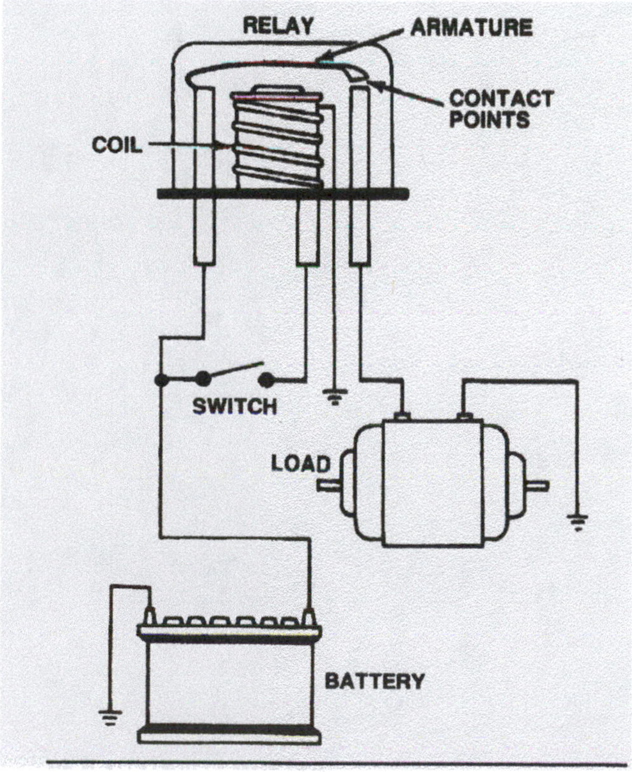
RELAY
ARMATURE
CONTACT POINTS
COIL
SWITCH
LOAD
BATTERY

_____ **3.** Check service information to determine the specified diagnostic procedure to follow to correctly diagnose a fault in a blower motor circuit.

____

____

____

____

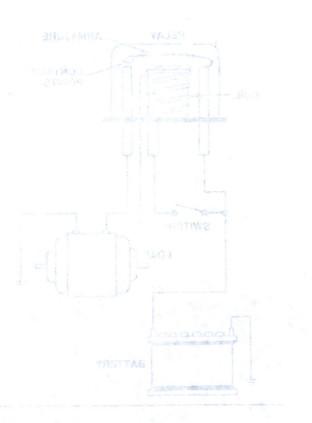

Locate Shorts, Grounds, and Opens

Meets NATEF Task: (A6-A-4) Locate shorts, ground, and opens; determine the necessary action. (P-1)

Name ______________________ **Date** __________ **Time on Task** __________

Make/Model ______________________ **Year** __________ **Evaluation: 4 3 2 1**

_____ **1.** Check service information for the recommended method for locating shorts, grounds, and opens.

____

____

_____ **2.** Follow the recommended troubleshooting procedure to locate the short-to-ground. Check all that apply.

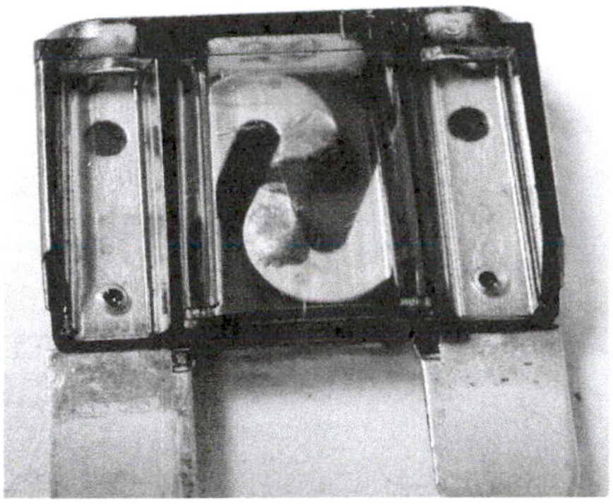

____ Short finder

____ Ohmmeter attached to the fuse panel with the fuse removed

____ Voltmeter attached to the fuse panel with the fuse removed

____ Ammeter attached to the fuse panel with the fuse removed

____ Sonic short finder

____ Other (describe) _______

_____ **3.** Most diagnostic test procedures include checking for proper power and ground at the component that is not functioning.

a. Is there voltage at the component when the circuit is activated?
Yes ____ **No** ____

b. Is there continuity between the ground connection at the component and a good chassis ground?
Yes ____ **No** ____

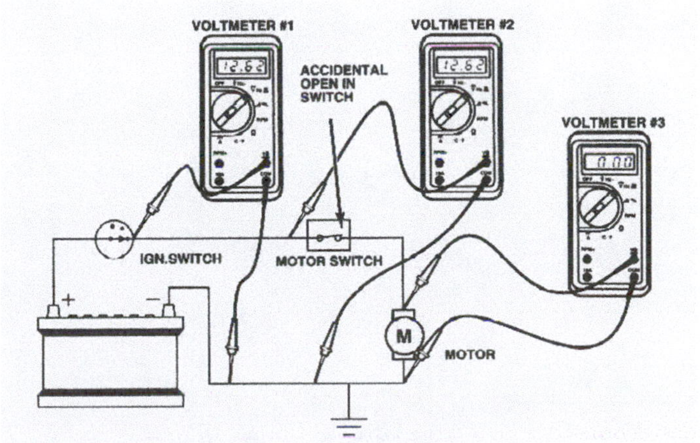
VOLTMETER #1
VOLTMETER #2
VOLTMETER #3
ACCIDENTAL OPEN IN SWITCH
IGN.SWITCH
MOTOR SWITCH
MOTOR
M

_____ **4.** Based on the test results, what is the necessary action? _______________

____

Blower Motor Radio Noise

Meets NATEF Task: (A6-H-11) Diagnose static and weak or no reception; determine necessary action (P-3)

Name ______________________ **Date** __________ **Time on Task** __________

Make/Model ______________________ **Year** __________ **Evaluation: 4 3 2 1**

A digital meter set to read AC volts can be used to easily check the capacitor connected to the blower motor. A blower motor generates an AC voltage as it rotates; the purpose and function of the capacitor attached to the positive power lead is to eliminate potential radio noise that could be created by the blower motor. To check to see if the capacitor is okay, follow these easy steps:

Step 1 Set a digital multimeter to read AC volts.

Step 2 Use a T-pin and carefully back probe the power lead at the blower motor being careful not to pierce the insulation. (The T-pin should just touch the metal terminal inside the plastic connection.)

Step 3 Connect one lead (with AC volts, it doesn't matter which lead is connected to which terminal) to the T-pin and the other lead to a good engine or body ground.

Step 4 Turn the blower on while observing the meter display. Check the AC voltage at all blower speeds.

Low = ________
Medium = ________
Medium high = ________
High = ________

The capacitor, blower motor, and wiring are okay if the AC voltage is less than 0.5 volt (500 mV).

OK _____ **NOT OK** _____

What is the necessary action? ____

____

We Support NATEF

Inspect and Test the Relays

Meets NATEF Task: (A6-A-10) Inspect and test switches, connectors, relays, and wires; determine the necessary action. (P-1)

Name ______________________ **Date** __________ **Time on Task** __________

Make/Model ______________________ **Year** __________ **Evaluation: 4 3 2 1**

_____ **1.** Check service information for the specified procedures for inspecting and testing relays.

____

____

_____ **2.** Relays should "click" when actuated. List all of the relays and determine if they click by listening or feeling the relay housing.

Circuit or Relay ID	Clicks? Yes or No
______________________	_______
______________________	_______
______________________	_______
______________________	_______
______________________	_______
______________________	_______

_____ **3.** How many four-terminal relays are used? ____________

_____ **4.** How many five-terminal relays are used? ____________

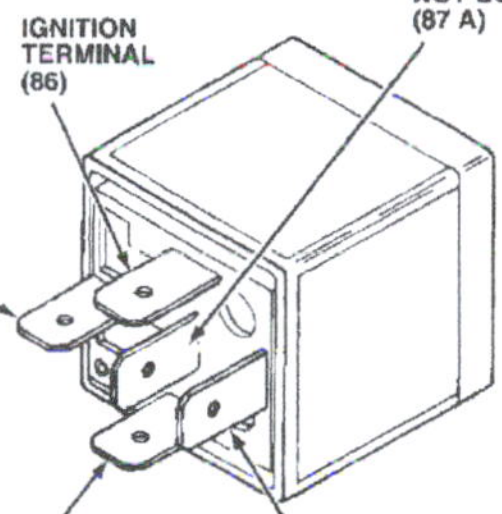
NOT USED
(87 A)
IGNITION
TERMINAL
(86)
BATTERY
TERMINAL
(30)
GROUND
(85)
SOLENOID
TERMINAL
(87)

_____ **5.** Test a relay for proper operation using an ohmmeter:

Coil resistance (usually labeled terminals 86 and 85) = ________ (usually between 60 and 100 ohms).

Continuity normally closed (NC) contact (usually labeled terminals 30 and 87) = ________ (should be close to zero ohms).

_____ **6.** Based on the inspections and tests, what is the necessary action? ________________

____

Electronic Fundamentals

Meets NATEF Task: Not specified by NATEF

Name ______________________ **Date** __________ **Time on Task** __________

Make/Model ______________________ **Year** __________ **Evaluation: 4 3 2 1**

_____ **1.** Describe the difference between a zener diode and a clamping diode. ____________

____

____

_____ **2.** Describe the operation of a photo resistor. ____________________

____

____

_____ **3.** What is meant by the term "negative coefficient thermistor?" ____________

____

____

_____ **4.** What is the difference between a PNP and a NPN transistor?

____

____

____

____

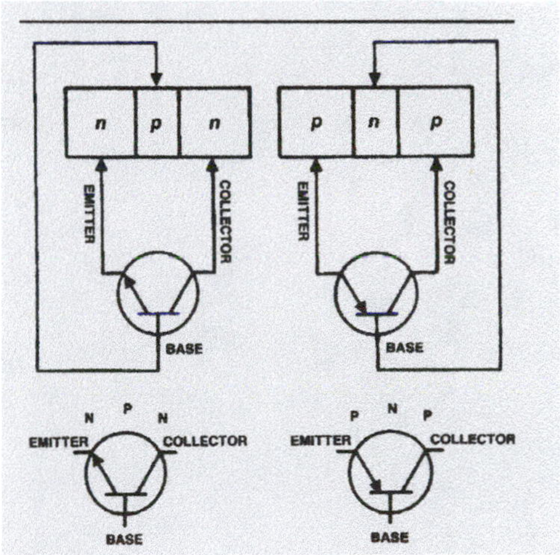

n
p
n
p
n
p
EMITTER
COLLECTOR
BASE
N
P
N
P
N
P

_____ **5.** List three precautions that service technicians should do to help prevent damage to electronic components from ESD.

a. ______________________________

b. ______________________________

c. ______________________________

We Support NATEF

PCM Actuators Diagnosis

Meets NATEF Task: (A8-B-3) Inspect and test computerized engine control system sensors, PCM/ECM, actuators, and circuits using a GMM/DSO; perform necessary action. (P-1)

Name ______________________ **Date** __________ **Time on Task** __________

Make/Model ______________________ **Year** __________ **Evaluation: 4 3 2 1**

_____ **1.** Check service information for the specified method and procedures to follow to check for proper operation of PCM-controlled actuators.

____

____

_____ **2.** Check all that apply:

TECH 2

___ Use a factory scan tool.

___ Use a generic OBD-II scan tool.

___ Use a DMM to check for resistance on communication circuits.

___ Use a fused jumper wire and a scan tool to diagnose communication errors.

___ Other (describe) ______________________________

_____ **3.** List the actuators that can be tested.

a. ____________________ f. ____________________

b. ____________________ g. ____________________

c. ____________________ h. ____________________

d. ____________________ j. ____________________

e. ____________________ k. ____________________

_____ **4.** Based on the test results, what is the necessary action? ____________________

____

Module Communication

Meets NATEF Task: (A8-H-7) Check for module communication errors using a scan tool. (P-2)

Name ____________________ **Date** __________ **Time on Task** __________

Make/Model ____________________ **Year** __________ **Evaluation: 4 3 2 1**

_____ **1.** Check service information for the specified method and procedures to follow to check for proper module communications.

____

____

_____ **2.** Check all that apply:

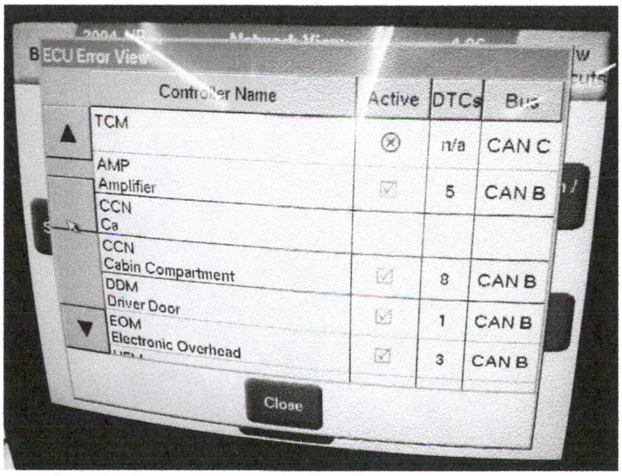
ECU Error View
Active
DTCs
TCM
n/a
CAN C
AMP
Amplifier
5
CAN B
CCN
Ca
CCN
Cabin Compartment
8
CAN B
DDM
Driver Door
1
CAN B
EOM
Electronic Overhead
3
CAN B
Close

___ Use a factory scan tool.

___ Use a global OBD-II scan tool.

___ Use a DMM to check for resistance on communication circuits.

___ Use a fused jumper wire and a scan tool to diagnose communication errors.

___ Other (describe) ______________________________

_____ **3.** List the modules that are preset in the vehicle being tested.

a. ____________________ f. ____________________

b. ____________________ g. ____________________

c. ____________________ h. ____________________

d. ____________________ j. ____________________

e. ____________________ k. ____________________

_____ **4.** Based on the test results, what is the necessary action? ____________________

____

Battery Specifications

Meets NATEF Task: Not specified by NATEF

Name ______________________ **Date** __________ **Time on Task** __________

Make/Model ______________________ **Year** __________ **Evaluation:** **4 3 2 1**

_____ **1.** Determine the following information about the battery.

A. Cold cranking amperes (CCA) rating = ______ (usually 500-1000)

B. Cranking amperes (CA) rating = ______ (usually 500-1000)

C. Reserve capacity rating (in minutes) = ______ (usually 50-200)

_____ **2.** What are the recommended load test amperes?

_______ A (normally 1/2 of CCA rating)

_____ **3.** Size of the battery:

Height = __________

Length = __________

Width = __________

Delco 60
550 COLD CRANKING AMPS
680 CRANKING AMPS
270 LOAD TEST AMPS
70-60S
DANGER EXPLOSIVE GASES
HYDROMETER

_____ **4.** Type of terminals:

_____ Side terminals

_____ Top terminals

_____ Both side and top terminals

_____ **5.** Determine the age of the battery from the shipping date sticker or other codes.

Sticker = ____________________

_____ Less than 1 year old

_____ 1 to 3 years old

_____ 3 to 5 years old

_____ Older than 5 years

_____ Unknown

Key Off Battery Drain

Meets NATEF Task: (A6-A-8) Measure and diagnose the cause(s) of excessive key-off battery drain (parasitic draw); determine the necessary action. (P-1)

Name ______________________ **Date** __________ **Time on Task** __________

Make/Model ______________________ **Year** __________ **Evaluation: 4 3 2 1**

A battery electrical drain test should be performed if a battery is dead (discharged) to determine if a battery electrical drain was the cause of the dead battery.

_____ **1.** Perform a visual inspection and check if the following are turned on:

a. The glove box light (instrument panel compartment light)
b. The interior light switch
c. Vanity mirror(s) light(s)
d. Trunk light (look for discoloration indicating that the bulb may have been on for a long time)

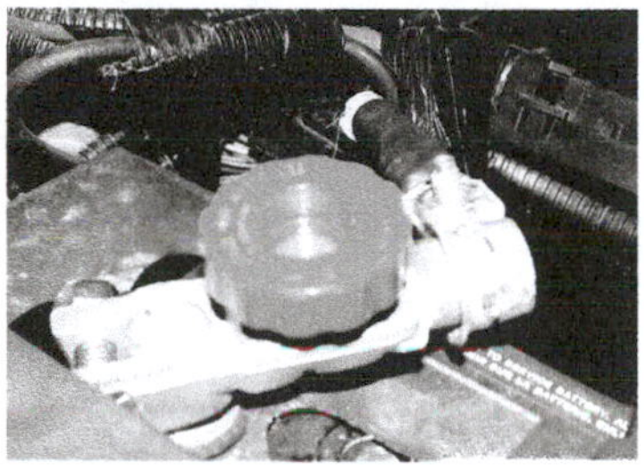

_____ **2.** Turn the ignition and all accessories off. Close all doors and the trunk. Disconnect the under-the-hood lamp if equipped.

_____ **3.** Disconnect the negative (-) battery cable.

_____ **4.** Select DC amperes on a digital multimeter.

_____ **5.** Connect the black meter lead to the negative terminal of the battery.

_____ **6.** Connect the red meter lead to the disconnected cable end and read the ammeter.

______ amps of battery electrical drain [should be less than 0.05A (50 mA)]

OK _____ **NOT OK** _____

_____ **7.** What is the necessary action? ________________________________

____

_____ **8.** Reconnect the battery, reset the radio presets, and set the time on the vehicle clock.

HINT: If possible, use a clip-on type digital multimeter or an amp probe to measure the battery drain. Using this equipment prevents the need to disconnect the battery cable and then have to reset the radio and the clock.

Battery and Capacity Tests

Meets NATEF Task: (A6-B-1 and A6-B-2) Perform battery state-of-charge test; determine necessary action. (P-1)

Name ______________________ **Date** __________ **Time on Task** __________

Make/Model ______________________ **Year** __________ **Evaluation: 4 3 2 1**

_____ **1.** Check service information for the specified method for determining the state-of-charge of the battery.

____

____

____

_____ **2.** Determine the state-of-charge using a voltmeter.

12.6 volts or higher	=	100% charged
12.4 volts	=	75% charged
12.2 volts	=	50% charged
12.0 volts	=	25% charged
10.5 volts	=	dead

_____ **3.** Determine the state-of-charge and capacity using a conductance tester.

____

_____ **4.** Determine the capacity of the battery using a carbon pile tester.

____

_____ **5.** What is the condition of the battery? ______________________________

_____ **6.** What is the necessary action? ______________________________

____

Electronic Memory Saver Usage

Meets NATEF Task: (A6-B-3) Maintain or restore electronic memory functions. (P-1)

Name ______________________ **Date** __________ **Time on Task** __________

Make/Model ______________________ **Year** __________ **Evaluation: 4 3 2 1**

_____ **1.** Check service information for the specified method and tools or equipment needed to maintain or restore electronic memory function.

____

____

____

_____ **2.** Most domestic brand vehicles can use the cigarette (auxiliary outlet) to apply voltage when the battery of the vehicle is removed or disconnected furring service. For this procedure to work, the lighter or auxiliary outlet must be powered with the ignition switch in the on position.

a. Using a DMM set to read DC volts, check for battery voltage at the lighter socket with the ignition off. ____**OK** ____**NOT OK**

b. Check for DC volts at the lighter socket with the ignition set to the on (run) position. ____ **OK** ____ **NOT OK**

_____ **3.** If the vehicle is equipped with a to-post-type battery design, a jump box can be attached to the ends of the cables to keep the memory in the electronic components while the battery is removed. Is this a possible method?

____ **Yes** ____ **No**

_____ **4.** Describe the method recommended to restore lost memory. __________________

____

____

Service and Replace the Battery

Meets NATEF Task: (A6-B-4) Inspect, clean, fill, and replace the battery. (P-2)

Name ______________________ **Date** __________ **Time on Task** __________

Make/Model ______________________ **Year** __________ **Evaluation:** 4 3 2 1

_____ **1.** Check service information for the specified procedures to follow to inspect, clean, fill, and replace a battery.

____

____

_____ **2.** Check all that apply:

____ Battery hold-down clamps/brackets are in place

____ Filler cap(s) is removable

____ Battery electrolyte cannot be checked

____ Electrolyte level is low

____ Corrosion was found on battery terminals/cable ends

____ Other faults or conditions (describe)

____

____

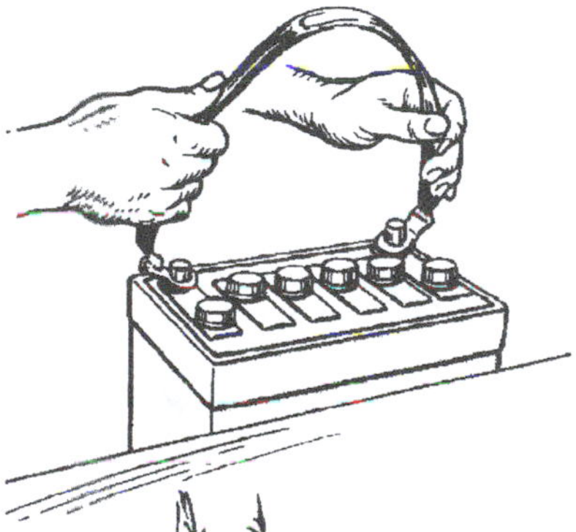

_____ **3.** Clean the battery.

_____ **4.** Clean the battery cables and cable ends.

_____ **5.** Remove and install the battery.

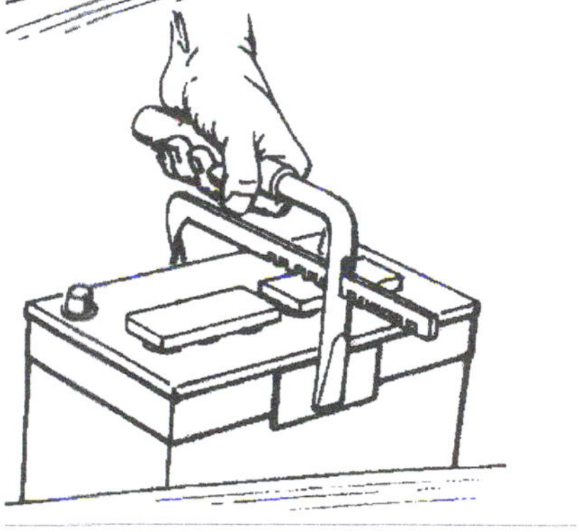

Battery Charging

Meets NATEF Task: (A6-B-5) Perform slow/fast battery charge. (P-2)

Name ________________ **Date** ________ **Time on Task** ________

Make/Model ________________ **Year** ________ **Evaluation: 4 3 2 1**

_____ **1.** Measure the open-circuit voltage of the battery = ______ volts (red lead of the voltmeter to positive [+] and black lead to negative [-]). (If more than 12.6 V, remove the surface charge by turning on the headlights for 1 minute).

_____ **2.** Percentage of charge = ______%.

12.6 V or higher	=	100% charged
12.4 V	=	75% charged
12.2 V	=	50% charged
12.0 V	=	25% charged
below 11.9 V	=	discharged

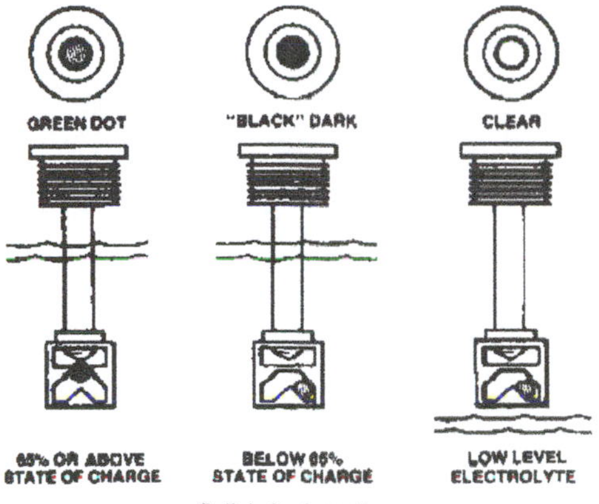
GREEN DOT
"BLACK" DARK
CLEAR
65% OR ABOVE STATE OF CHARGE
BELOW 65% STATE OF CHARGE
LOW LEVEL ELECTROLYTE
Built-in hydrometer.

_____ **3.** Determine the cold cranking amperes (CCA) of the battery = __________.

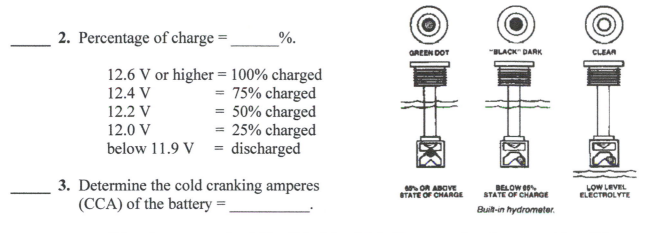

(*The charge rate should be 1% of the CCA.* For example, a battery with a 500 CCA rating should be charged at 5 ampere rate.) Charge Rate = $\frac{CCA}{100}$

_____ **4.** Determine the reserve capacity in minutes = _________.

(*The charge rate can be determined by dividing the reserve capacity of the battery in minutes by 30.* For example, a 180-minute battery should be charged at 6 ampere rate: 180/30 = 6).

$$\text{Charge Rate} = \frac{\text{Reserve Capacity}}{30}$$

_____ **5.** The battery should be charged at _____ amperes (CCA method) or at _____ amperes (reserve capacity method).

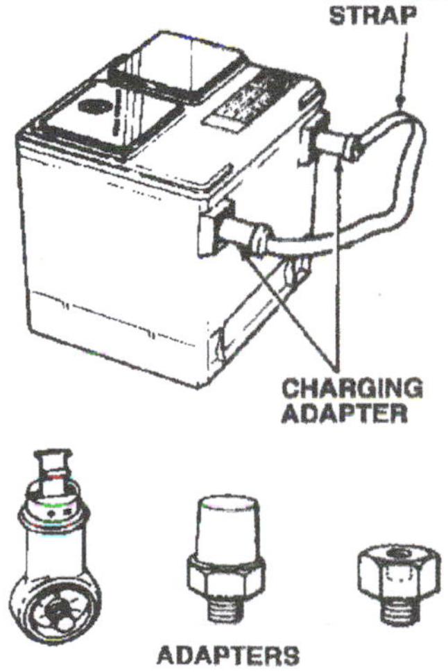
INSULATOR STRAP
CHARGING ADAPTER
ADAPTERS

Jump Starting

Meets NATEF Task: (A6-B-6) Start a vehicle using jumper cables and a battery or auxiliary power supply. (P-1)

Name ______________________ **Date** __________ **Time on Task** __________

Make/Model ______________________ **Year** __________ **Evaluation:** 4 3 2 1

_____ **1.** Move the good vehicle to within reach of the jumper cables of the disabled vehicle (or use a portable jumper box).

_____ **2.** Check that the ignition is in the "off" position on both vehicles.

_____ **3.** Connect the jumper cables in the following order:

a. Red cable ends to the positive (+) terminals of both batteries
b. One black cable end to the negative (-) terminal of the good vehicle
c. The other black cable end to a good, unpainted engine ground at least one foot from the battery

_____ **4.** Start the good vehicle.

_____ **5.** Allow the good vehicle to run for several minutes to charge the battery of the disabled vehicle.

_____ **6.** Start the disabled vehicle.

_____ **7.** After the engine is running smoothly, disconnect the black cable from the engine ground of the disabled vehicle and then disconnect the negative terminal of the battery of the good vehicle.

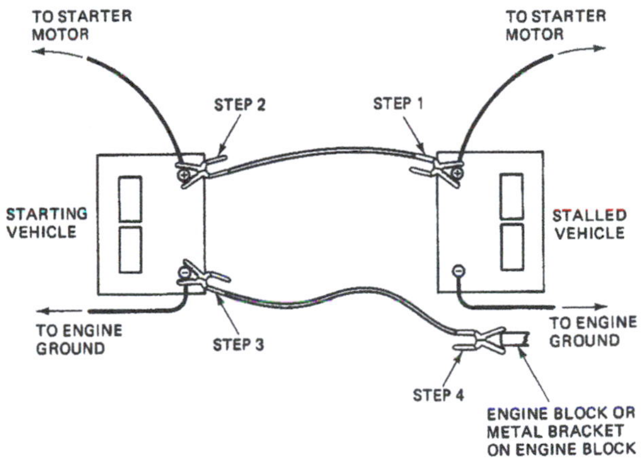
TO STARTER MOTOR
TO STARTER MOTOR
STEP 2
STEP 1
STARTING VEHICLE
STALLED VEHICLE
TO ENGINE GROUND
STEP 3
TO ENGINE GROUND
STEP 4
ENGINE BLOCK OR METAL BRACKET ON ENGINE BLOCK

_____ **8.** Disconnect the red battery cable ends from the positive terminals of the batteries.

Reinitialization

Meets NATEF Task: (A6-B-8) Identify electronic modules that require reinitialization or code entry following a battery disconnect. (P-2)

Name ______________________________ **Date** __________ **Time on Task** __________

Make/Model ________________________ **Year** _________ **Evaluation: 4 3 2 1**

_____ **1.** Check service information for the electronic modules or components such as security radios that require reinitialization or code entry following a battery disconnect. Check all that apply.

_____ Radio

_____ Power windows

_____ Power doors/taillights

_____ Remote keyless entry

_____ Security system

_____ Other (specify) ____

_____ **2.** What is the necessary action to reinitialize the electronic module?

	Required procedure (in code entry)
Radio	________________________________
Security system	________________________________
Remote keyless entry	________________________________
Power windows	________________________________
Power doors/taillights	________________________________
Security system	________________________________
Other ______________	________________________________

Hybrid Auxiliary Battery

Meets NATEF Task: (A6-B-9) Identify hybrid vehicle auxiliary (12V) battery service and test procedures. (P-3)

Name ______________________ **Date** __________ **Time on Task** __________

Make/Model ______________________ **Year** __________ **Evaluation:** 4 3 2 1

_____ **1.** Check service information for the location of the hybrid vehicle auxiliary (12V) battery, if equipped. ______________________________

____

____

MAINTENANCE FREE BATTE

_____ **2.** What are the battery specifications? CCA = ______ Size = _________

_____ **3.** Describe the service procedures: ______________________________

____

____

_____ **4.** Based on the specified test results, what is the necessary action? ____________

____

____

We Support NATEF

Cranking System Identification

Meets NATEF Task: Not specified by NATEF

Name ______________________ **Date** __________ **Time on Task** __________

Make/Model ______________________ **Year** __________ **Evaluation: 4 3 2 1**

_____ **1.** Locate the battery and describe its location: ______________________

____

_____ **2.** Check service information and determine the location of the ignition switch (**not** the ignition lock assembly) and describe its location. ______________________

____

_____ **3.** Check service information and determine the location of the starter solenoid.

_____ Attached to the starter motor

_____ Remotely mounted (describe the location) ______________

____

_____ **4.** What is the color of the wire from the ignition start (crank) position on the ignition switch to the starter solenoid "S" terminal? ______________________

_____ **5.** Describe the location of the starter motor. ______________________

____

_____ **6.** After checking the service information, list the steps necessary to remove the starter motor.

1. ______________________
2. ______________________
3. ______________________
4. ______________________
5. ______________________
6. ______________________
7. ______________________
8. ______________________

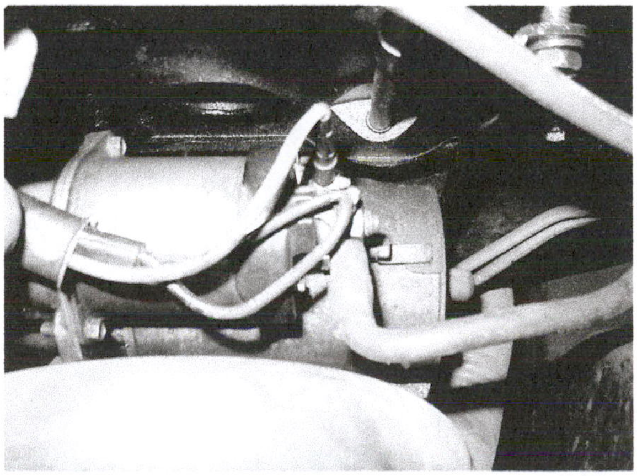

Starter Disassembly and Testing

Meets NATEF Task: Not specified by NATEF

Name ______________________________ **Date** __________ **Time on Task** __________

Make/Model ________________________ **Year** _________ **Evaluation: 4 3 2 1**

_____ **1.** Clean and visually inspect the starter for physical damage such as a cracked or broken drive-end housing.

OK _____ **NOT OK** _____

_____ **2.** Mark the location of the through bolts on the frame housing and make note of the location of a special through bolt used to retain a support bracket.

_____ used a support bracket _____ did not use a support bracket

_____ **3.** Remove the solenoid (if it is a solenoid activated-type starter).

CAUTION: When removing the solenoid, use caution because the plunger return spring may cause the solenoid to be forced away from the starter when the attaching bolts (nuts) are removed.

_____ **4.** Remove the through bolts.

_____ **5.** Gently remove the brush-end housing and armature from the field housing.

_____ **6.** Remove the shift fork and separate the drive-end housing from the field housing.

_____ **7.** Visually inspect all the parts and note their condition.

armature	**OK** ___	**NOT OK** ___	**Notes:** __________
brushes/holders	**OK** ___	**NOT OK** ___	**Notes:** __________
field coils	**OK** ___	**NOT OK** ___	**Notes:** __________
drive-end housing	**OK** ___	**NOT OK** ___	**Notes:** __________
shift lever	**OK** ___	**NOT OK** ___	**Notes:** __________

_____ **8.** Set the multimeter to read ohms and check the resistance between the hot brushes and the field housing (should read OL).

OK _____ **NOT OK** _____

_____ **9.** Check the armature on a growler for opens and shorts.

OK _____ **NOT OK** _____

Starter Solenoid Testing

Meets NATEF Task: Not specified by NATEF

Name ______________________________ **Date** __________ **Time on Task** __________

Make/Model ________________________ **Year** _________ **Evaluation: 4 3 2 1**

_____ **1.** Clean and visually inspect the starter solenoid for physical damage.

OK _____ **NOT OK** _____

_____ **2.** Carefully remove the two retaining screws and the retaining nuts from the "M", "S", and "R" (if used) terminals.

_____ **3.** Carefully remove the plastic end cap.

_____ **4.** Visually check all solenoid parts for excessive wear or damage.

OK _____ **NOT OK** _____

_____ **5.** Set a digital multimeter (DMM) to read ohms (low scale) and check the hold-in coil and the pull-in coil.

Pull-in coil. Measure between terminals "S" and "M":
resistance = ______ (should be 0.2 to 0.4 ohm) **OK** _____ **NOT OK** _____

Hold-in coil. Measure between terminals "S" and the solenoid housing:
resistance = _______ (should be 0.4 to 0.6 ohm) **OK** _____ **NOT OK** _____

_____ **6.** Carefully reassemble the solenoid.

_____ **7.** Test the pull-in winding by applying 12 volts to terminal "S" and ground to terminal "M." Check that the plunger will be drawn into the solenoid.

CAUTION: The plunger will be drawn in with great force, so keep your fingers away from between the plunger and the solenoid housing.

OK _____ **NOT OK** _____

_____ **8.** Check the hold-in winding by connecting 12 volts to terminal "S" and the other wire to ground. The plunger should be drawn into the solenoid housing.

OK _____ **NOT OK** _____

_____ **9.** Based on the test results, what is the necessary action? ______________________________

____

We Support NATEF

Starter Voltage Drop/Current Draw Tests

Meets NATEF Task: (A6-C-1, A6-C-2, and A6-C-6) Perform starter current draw tests; determine necessary action. (P-1)

Name ______________________ **Date** __________ **Time on Task** __________

Make/Model ______________________ **Year** __________ **Evaluation: 4 3 2 1**

_____ **1.** Check service information for the specified starter current draw test procedure and specifications.

____

____

NOTE: Few vehicle manufacturers give starter current draw specifications with the starter installed on the vehicle. Use the chart below as a guideline regarding the range of the maximum allowable starter draw.

4-cylinder engines = 150 to 185 amperes maximum (normally less than 100 A)
6-cylinder engines = 160 to 200 amperes maximum (normally less than 125 A)
8-cylinder engines = 185 to 250 amperes maximum (normally less than 150 A)

_____ **2.** Perform the starter current draw test following the manufacturer's instructions.

Results: ________ amperes

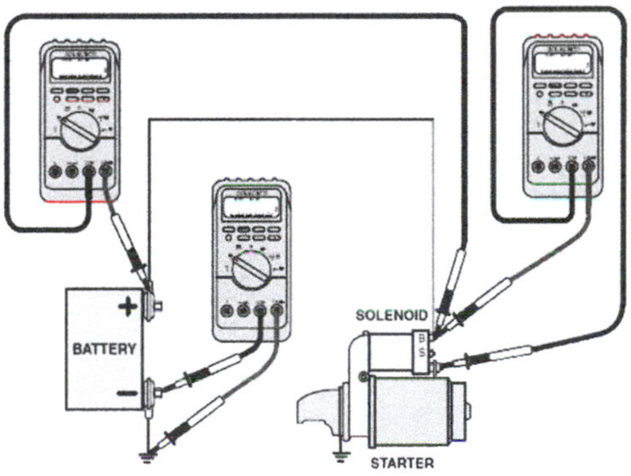
BATTERY
SOLENOID
STARTER

_____ **3.** Connect the voltmeter, as shown in the illustration, and crank the engine. Observe the voltmeter.

_____ **4.** All test results should be less than 0.2 V (200 mV).

_____ **5.** Based on the specifications and the test results, what is the necessary action?

____

____

____

____

Starter Relays and Solenoids

Meets NATEF Task: (A6-C-3 and A6-C-5) Inspect and test starter relays, solenoids, connections, and wires; determine necessary action. (P-2)

Name ______________________ **Date** __________ **Time on Task** __________

Make/Model ______________________ **Year** __________ **Evaluation: 4 3 2 1**

_____ **1.** Clean and visually inspect the starter solenoid and/or relay for physical damage.

OK _____ **NOT OK** _____

_____ **2.** Set a digital multimeter (DMM) to read ohms (low scale) and check the hold-in coil and the pull-in coil.

Pull-in coil. Measure between terminals "S" and "M":
resistance = ______ (should be 0.2 to 0.4 ohm) **OK** _____ **NOT OK** _____

Hold-in coil. Measure between terminals "S" and the solenoid housing:
resistance = _______ (should be 0.4 to 0.6 ohm) **OK** _____ **NOT OK** _____

_____ **3.** Test the pull-in winding by applying 12 volts to terminal "S" and ground to terminal "M." Check that the plunger will be drawn into the solenoid.

OK _____ **NOT OK** _____

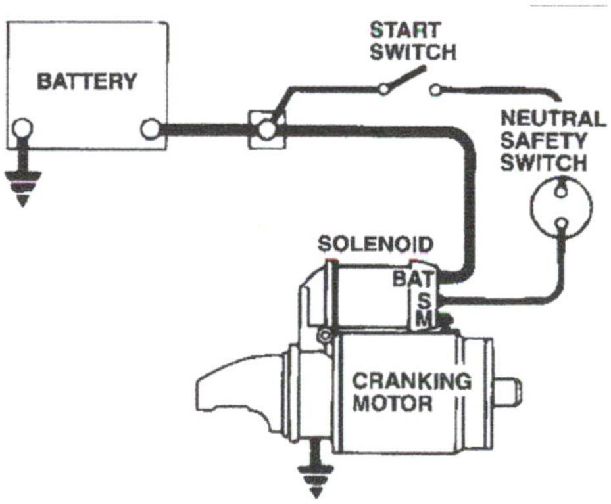

BATTERY
START SWITCH
NEUTRAL SAFETY SWITCH
SOLENOID
BAT
S
M
CRANKING MOTOR

_____ **4.** Check the hold-in winding by connecting 12 volts to terminal "S" and the other wire to ground. The plunger should be drawn into the solenoid housing.

OK _____ **NOT OK** _____

_____ **5.** Measure coil resistance of the relay (terminals 86 and 85).

Resistance = ______ ohms
(should be 60 to 100 ohms)

OK _____ **NOT OK** _____

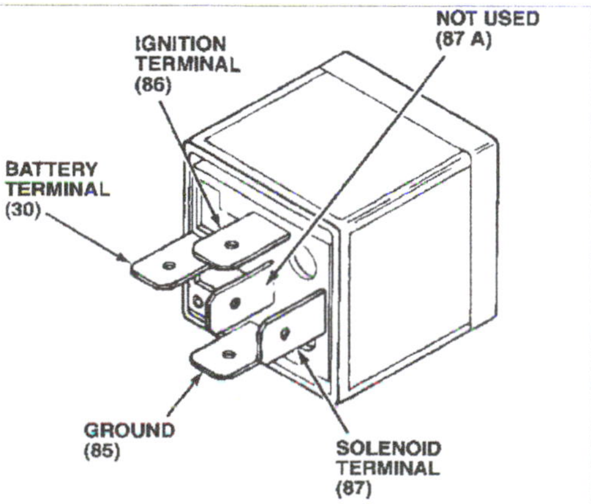

IGNITION TERMINAL (86)
NOT USED (87 A)
BATTERY TERMINAL (30)
GROUND (85)
SOLENOID TERMINAL (87)

_____ **6.** What is the necessary action?

____

____

We Support NATEF

Remove and Install the Starter

Meets NATEF Task: (A6-C-4) Remove and install starter in a vehicle. (P-1)

Name ______________________ **Date** __________ **Time on Task** __________

Make/Model ______________________ **Year** __________ **Evaluation:** **4 3 2 1**

_____ **1.** Check service information for the specified procedures for the removal and installation of a starter in a vehicle.

____

____

____

____

_____ **2.** Does the service information require that the battery be disconnected?
___ **Yes** ___ **No**

_____ **3.** What are the torque specifications for the starter fasteners? ______________________

____

_____ **4.** What are the torque specifications for the wiring connectors? ____________________

____

_____ **5.** Show the instructor the starter removed from the vehicle. **Instructor's OK** _______

_____ **6.** Show the instructor the starter installed in the vehicle. **Instructor's OK** _______

Alternator Identification

Meets NATEF Task: Not specified by NATEF

Name ______________________ **Date** __________ **Time on Task** __________

Make/Model ______________________ **Year** __________ **Evaluation: 4 3 2 1**

_____ **1.** Locate the alternator and describe the location. ____________________

____

_____ **2.** Check service information and determine the maximum amperage output and charging system voltage.

- Amperage rating (usually ranges from 60 A to 160 A) __________
- Charging system voltage (usually within 13.5 to 15.0 volts) __________

_____ **3.** Locate the alternator and identify which wire(s) supply electrical power to the vehicle electrical system and battery.

- Color of power lead wire(s) ______________________
- Wire gauge of the power lead wire(s) ________________

_____ **4.** What type of electrical protection is included in the alternator output circuit?

_____ Fusible link (describe location) ______________________

_____ Maximum fuse (rating = ______________)

Describe location ______________________

_____ Unknown

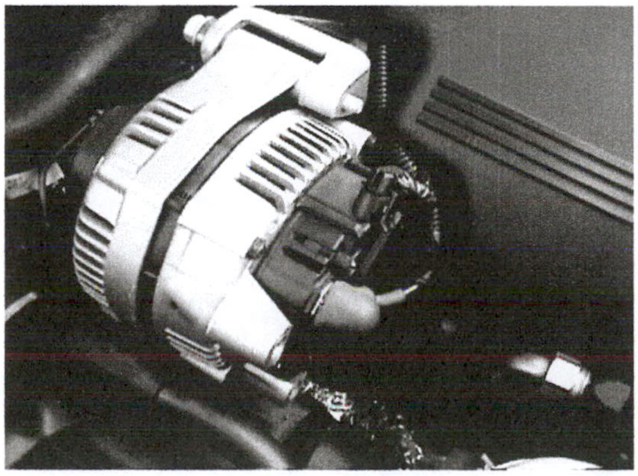

Alternator Disassembly

Meets NATEF Task: Not specified by NATEF

Name ______________________ **Date** __________ **Time on Task** __________

Make/Model ______________________ **Year** __________ **Evaluation:** 4 3 2 1

_____ **1.** Visually check the alternator for physical damage.

OK _____ **NOT OK** _____

_____ **2.** Use a marker or scribe to mark the case of the alternator so it can be correctly reassembled in the same "clock position."

_____ **3.** Remove the through bolts and separate the alternator.

NOTE: The laminations of the stator should be held against the rear half of the alternator.

_____ **4.** Remove the stator from the rectifier bridge.

_____ **5.** Remove the brushes and voltage regulator.

_____ **6.** Remove the rectifier bridge.

_____ **7.** Thoroughly clean and test the alternator parts before reassembly.

We Support NATEF

Alternator Rotor Testing

Meets NATEF Task: Not specified by NATEF

Name ______________________ **Date** __________ **Time on Task** __________

Make/Model ______________________ **Year** __________ **Evaluation: 4 3 2 1**

_____ **1.** Carefully inspect the rotor for damage.

OK _____ **NOT OK** _____

_____ **2.** Use 400 grit emery cloth to clean the slip rings. Be sure to rotate the slips in the cloth to avoid creating flat areas.

_____ **3.** Set a digital multimeter (DMM) to read ohms (low scale).

_____ **4.** Measure the resistance between the slip rings and compare with specifications:

actual = __________

GM	=	2.2 to 3.5 Ω
Ford	=	3.0 to 5.5 Ω
Chrysler	=	3.0 to 6.0 Ω

OK _____ **NOT OK** _____

_____ **5.** To test that the rotor winding is not shorted-to-ground, place one meter lead on a slip ring and the other meter lead to the steel shaft of the rotor. The reading should be infinity (OL) if the rotor is OK.

reading = ____________ **OK** _____ **NOT OK** _____

Shorted-to-ground

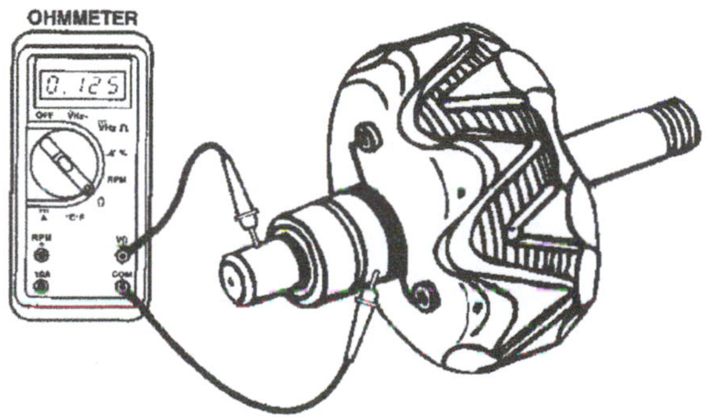
OHMMETER
0.125

Open

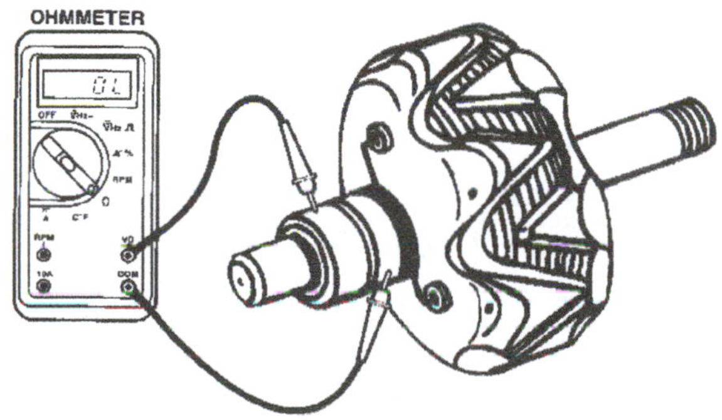
OHMMETER
OL

Alternator Stator Testing

Meets NATEF Task: Not specified by NATEF

Name ______________________________ **Date** __________ **Time on Task** _________

Make/Model ________________________ **Year** _________ **Evaluation:** 4 3 2 1

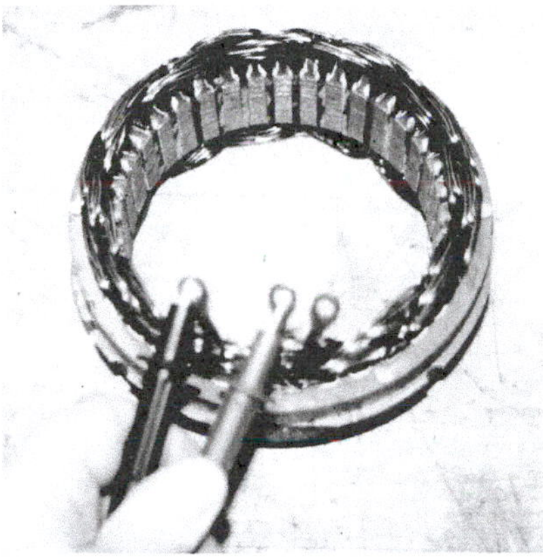

_____ **1.** Identify the type of stator.

_____ **Wye** (has three terminals with one wire at each terminal and a wire junction)

_____ **Delta** (has three terminals with two wires at each terminal)

_____ **2.** Visually inspect the rotor for faults such as burned insulation due to overheating or broken wires.

OK _____ **NOT OK** _____

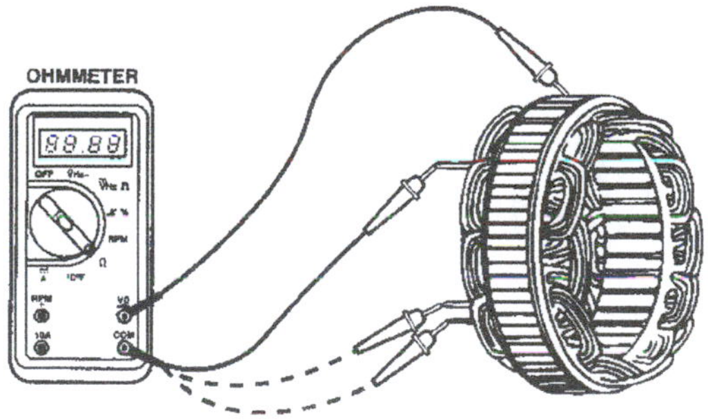
OHMMETER

_____ **3.** Set a digital multimeter to read ohms (low scale).

_____ **4.** Measure the resistance between all three terminals of the stator two at a time. The resistance will be low (usually less than 2 ohms). If high or infinity, the stator is defective.

OK _____ **NOT OK** _____

_____ **5.** To check if the stator windings are shorted-to-ground, connect one lead of the meter (still set to read ohms) to the steel laminations of the stator and touch the other lead to each of the three terminals. The reading on all three terminals should be infinity (OL).

OK _____ **NOT OK** _____

Alternator Rectifier Bridge Testing

Meets NATEF Task: Not specified by NATEF

Name ______________________ **Date** __________ **Time on Task** __________

Make/Model ______________________ **Year** __________ **Evaluation: 4 3 2 1**

_____ **1.** Identify the type of alternator.

_____ GM
_____ Ford
_____ Chrysler
_____ other (specify) ______________________

_____ **2.** How many diodes are used in the rectifier bridge (2 per stator winding)?

_____ 6
_____ 8
_____ other (specify) ______________

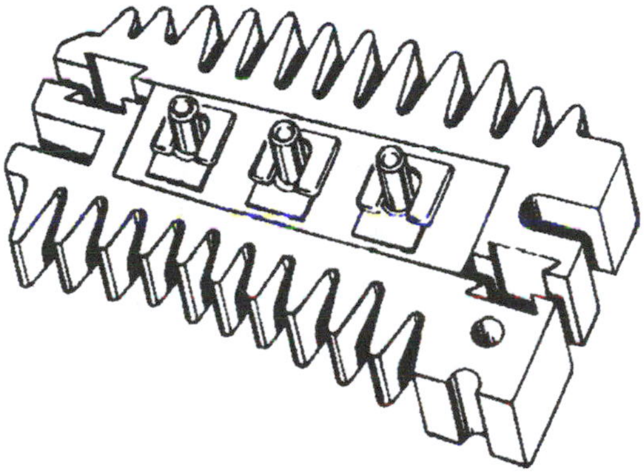

_____ **3.** Visually check the rectifier bridge for physical damage.

OK _____ **NOT OK** _____

_____ **4.** Set a digital multimeter to the diode check position.

_____ **5.** Touch one meter lead to the terminal of the diode and the other lead to the heat sink for the same diode and record the reading. Reverse the leads and record the second reading. A good diode should read infinity (OL) one way and record a voltage drop reading of between 0.4 volt (400 mV) and 0.6 volt (600 mV) the other way.

reading for diode #1 = __________ and __________
reading for diode #2 = __________ and __________
reading for diode #3 = __________ and __________
reading for diode #4 = __________ and __________
reading for diode #5 = __________ and __________
reading for diode #6 = __________ and __________

OK _____ **NOT OK** _____

_____ **6.** Test the diode trio (if equipped) in a similar manner. **OK** _____ **NOT OK** _____

Charging System Output Test

Meets NATEF Task: (A6-D-1) Perform charging system output test; determine necessary action. (P-1)

Name ________________ **Date** __________ **Time on Task** __________

Make/Model ________________ **Year** __________ **Evaluation: 4 3 2 1**

_____ **1.** Check service information for the specified charging system output test procedures and specifications.

____

_____ **2.** Connect the starting and charging test unit leads to the battery as per the manufacturer's instructions.

_____ **3.** Attach the amp probe around the alternator output wire.

_____ **4.** Start the engine and operate at 2,000 RPM (fast idle).

_____ **5.** Turn the "load increase" control slowly to obtain the highest reading on the ammeter scale. (Do not let the battery voltage drop to less than 12 volts.)
Tested amps = __________ amps.

_____ **6.** Specification (should be stamped on the alternator or indicated by a colored tag on or near the output terminal) = _________ amps.

_____ **7.** Results should be within 10% of the specifications. If the alternator amperage output is low, first check the condition of the alternator drive belt. The alternator should not be able to be rotated by hand with the engine "off."

OK_____ NOT OK_____

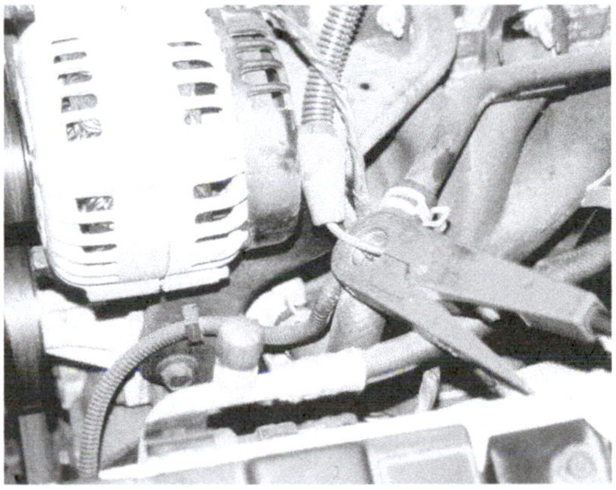

_____ **8.** Based on the results of the charging system output test, what is the necessary action?

____

____

Charging System Diagnosis

Meets NATEF Task: (A6-D-2) Diagnose charging systems for undercharge, no-charge, and overcharge conditions. (P-1)

Name ______________________________ **Date** __________ **Time on Task** __________

Make/Model ________________________ **Year** _________ **Evaluation:** 4 3 2 1

_____ **1.** Check service information for:

a. Specified charging system voltage specifications and testing procedures

____

b. Specified charging system voltage = ____________________

c. Specified charging system diagnostic procedure = ______________________

____

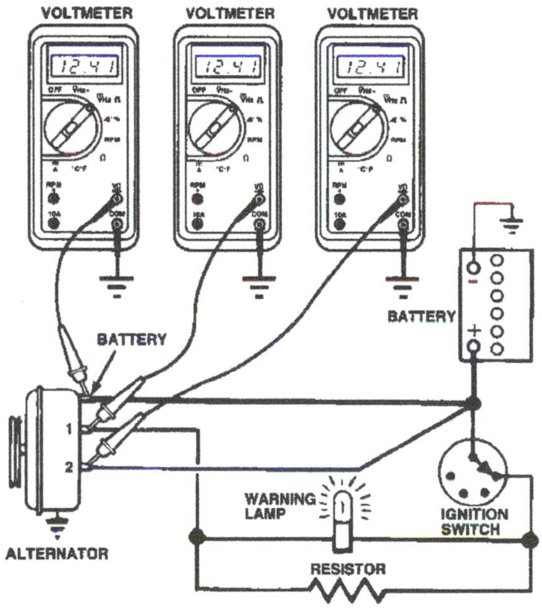
VOLTMETER
VOLTMETER
VOLTMETER
12.41
12.41
12.41
BATTERY
BATTERY
1
2
ALTERNATOR
WARNING LAMP
IGNITION SWITCH
RESISTOR

_____ **2.** Measure the charging system voltage = _______________.

_____ **3.** Measure the AC ripple voltage - ________ (should be less than 0.5 volt).

_____ **4.** Based on the test results, what is the necessary action? ________________________

____

Remove and Install Alternator

Meets NATEF Task: (A6-D-3 and A6-D-4) Remove, inspect, and install alternator. (P-1)

Name ______________________________ **Date** __________ **Time on Task** __________

Make/Model ________________________ **Year** __________ **Evaluation: 4 3 2 1**

_____ **1.** Check service information for the specified procedures for the removal and installation of a generator alternator in a vehicle.

____

____

____

____

____

56041693AA
TN121000-4410 12V
DENSO

_____ **2.** Does the service information require that the battery be disconnected? ___**Yes** ___ **No**

_____ **3.** What are the torque specifications for the alternator fasteners? _________

____

_____ **4.** What is the condition of the drive belt, pulley, and tensions? ___________________

____

_____ **5.** Show the instructor the alternator removed from the vehicle. **Instructor's OK** _____

_____ **6.** Show the instructor the alternator installed in the vehicle. **Instructor's OK** _____

We Support NATEF

Charging Circuit Voltage Drop

Meets NATEF Task: (A6-D-5) Perform charging circuit voltage drop tests; determine necessary action (P-1)

Name ______________________ **Date** __________ **Time on Task** __________

Make/Model ______________________ **Year** __________ **Evaluation: 4 3 2 1**

_____ **1.** Check service information for specified procedures and voltage drop specifications of the charging circuit.

_____ **2.** Connect one test lead of a digital multimeter set to read DC volts to the alternator output terminal and the positive (+) terminal of the battery.

_____ **3.** Start the engine and run to 2,000 RPM (fast idle).

_____ **4.** Turn on the headlights to force the alternator to charge the battery.

_____ **5.** The voltage drop reading should not exceed 0.40 volt.

_____ = the voltage drop of the *insulated* (power side) of the charging circuit (between the output terminal of the alternator and the positive (+) terminal of the battery).

OK_____ **NOT OK**_____

_____ **6.** To test if the generator is properly grounded, continue operating the engine at a fast idle with the lights on, connect the meter leads to the case of the generator and the negative (-) terminal of the battery. A reading of greater than 0.20 volt indicates a poor generator ground.

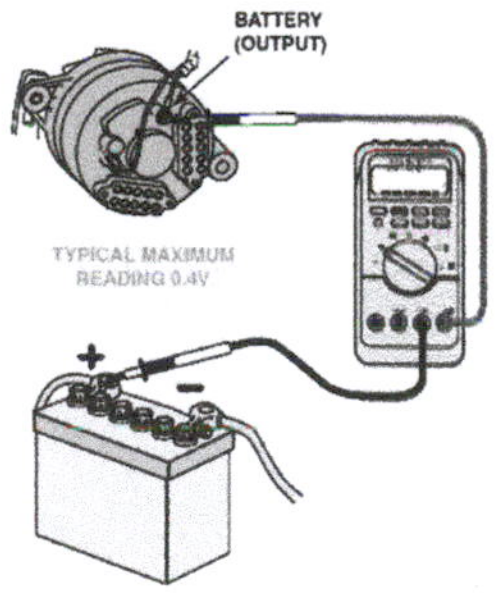
BATTERY (OUTPUT)
TYPICAL MAXIMUM READING 0.4V
+
-

VOLTAGE DROP - INSULATED CHARGING CIRCUIT

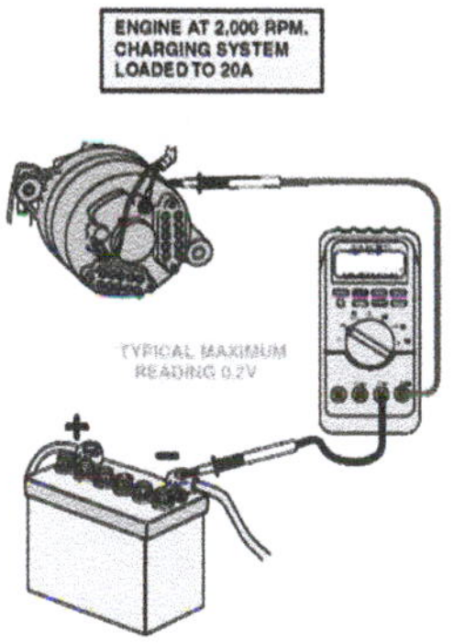
ENGINE AT 2,000 RPM. CHARGING SYSTEM LOADED TO 20A
TYPICAL MAXIMUM READING 0.2V
+
-

VOLTAGE DROP - CHARGING GROUND CIRCUIT

_____ = the voltage drop of the *ground side* of the alternator (between the rear housing of the alternator and the negative (-) terminal of the battery).

OK_____ **NOT OK**_____

_____ **7.** Based on the test results, what is the necessary action? ______________________

____

Lighting System Diagnosis

Meets NATEF Task: (A6-E-1, A6-E-2, and A6-E-3) Diagnose lighting concerns; determine necessary action. (P-1)

Name ______________________ **Date** __________ **Time on Task** __________

Make/Model ______________________ **Year** __________ **Evaluation: 4 3 2 1**

_____ **1.** Check service information for the specified lighting diagnosis procedures and specifications.

____

____

_____ **2.** What type of headlights are used on the vehicle?

____ Sealed beam
____ Halogen replacement bulbs
____ High-intensity discharge (HID)
____ Other (describe) ______________________

_____ **3.** Is alignment equipment needed? ___ **Yes** ___ **No**

If yes, describe: ______________________

_____ **4.** Is the headlight unit equipped with a bubble level? ___ **Yes** ___ **No**

_____ **5.** Is the correct bulb trade number installed? ___ **Yes** ___ **No**

_____ **6.** Check for proper power and ground at the socket of the bulb.

____ **OK** ____ **NOT OK** (describe fault) ______________

____

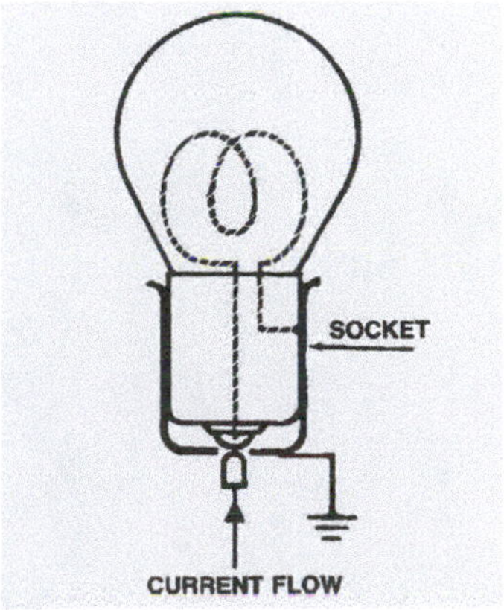
SOCKET
CURRENT FLOW

_____ **7.** Based on the inspection and testing, what is the necessary action?

____

____

High-Intensity Discharge Headlights

Meets NATEF Task: (A6-E-4) Identify system voltage and other precautions associated with HID headlights. (P-3)

Name ______________________ **Date** __________ **Time on Task** __________

Make/Model ______________________ **Year** __________ **Evaluation: 4 3 2 1**

_____ **1.** Check service information for the specified precautions when working with high-intensity discharge (HID) lights. The safety precautions include:

a. ____

b. ____

c. ____

_____ **2.** What is the voltage output of the HID ballast assembly? ______________

_____ **3.** What is the specified testing procedure for diagnosing faults with high-intensity discharge lighting systems?

Step 1: ____

Step 2: ____

Step 3: ____

Step 4: ____

_____ **4.** List the tools and test equipment needed to test high-intensity discharge headlight systems.

a. ______________________________

b. ______________________________

c. ______________________________

d. ______________________________

Gauge Diagnosis

Meets NATEF Task: (A6-F-1) Inspect and test gauges and gauge sending units; determine necessary action. (P-1)

Name ______________________________ **Date** __________ **Time on Task** __________

Make/Model ________________________ **Year** _________ **Evaluation:** **4 3 2 1**

_____ **1.** Locate the wiring schematic for the dash gauge circuits and determine the color of the wires.

Fuel gauge ___________, ___________, and ___________

Oil pressure coolant temperature __________, ___________, and __________

Color of wires to the sending unit: ______________ and ________________

_____ **2.** Check service information and determine the specified resistance of the sending unit when the gas tank is full and empty.

Full tank = ______________ Empty tank = ______________

_____ **3.** Determine the resistance specification of the sending unit.

Resistance of the sending unit when the oil pressure is high = ______________

Resistance of the sending unit when the oil pressure is low = _______________

_____ **4.** Determine the specified resistance of the sensor when hot and cold.

Resistance when the coolant is cold = ____________________________

Resistance when the coolant is hot = _____________________________

_____ **5.** Based on the tests, what is the necessary action?

____

____

____

____

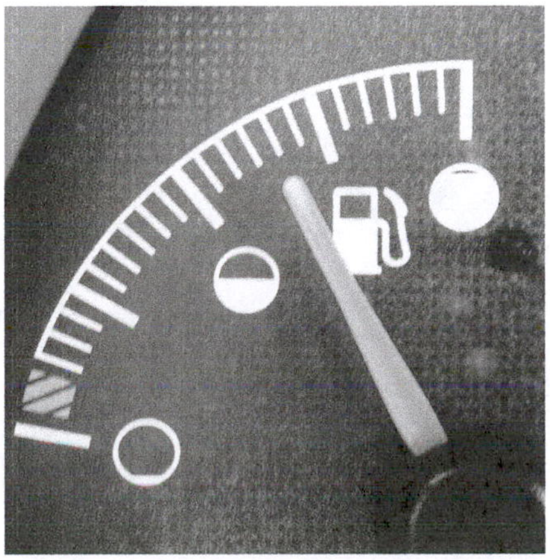

Driver Information and Warning Devices

Meets NATEF Task: (A6-F-2) Inspect and test connectors, wires, and printed circuit boards of gauge circuits; determine necessary action. (P-3)

Name ______________________ **Date** __________ **Time on Task** __________

Make/Model ______________________ **Year** __________ **Evaluation: 4 3 2 1**

_____ **1.** Check service information for the specified testing procedures to test the gauge printed circuit boards, and diagnosis of warning devices.______________________

____

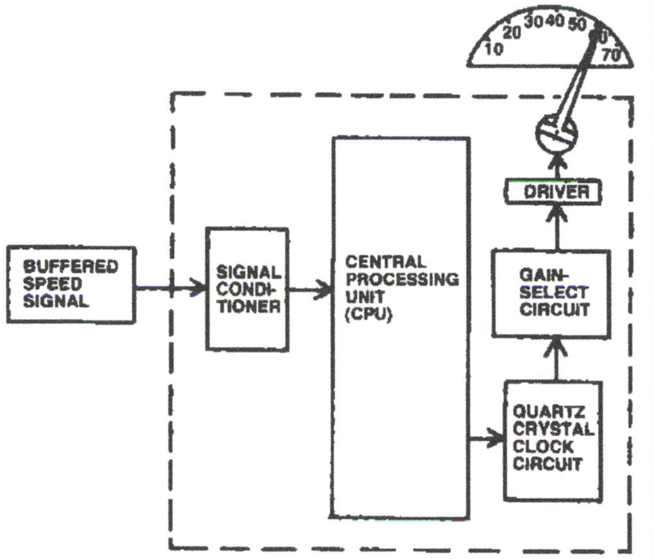
10
20
30
40
50
60
70
DRIVER
BUFFERED SPEED SIGNAL
SIGNAL CONDI-TIONER
CENTRAL PROCESSING UNIT (CPU)
GAIN-SELECT CIRCUIT
QUARTZ CRYSTAL CLOCK CIRCUIT

CLUSTER CIRCUIT

_____ **2.** Perform a visual inspection of the wires and connectors to the printed circuit boards.

____ **OK**

____ **NOT OK** (describe fault) ______________________

_____ **3.** Visually check the gauge printed circuit boards for discoloration or poor solder joints.

____ **OK**

____ **NOT OK**

_____ **4.** Based on the tests and inspection, what is the necessary action? ______________

____

Horn

Meets NATEF Task: (A6-G-1) Diagnose incorrect horn operation; perform necessary action. (P-2)

Name ______________________ **Date** __________ **Time on Task** __________

Make/Model ______________________ **Year** __________ **Evaluation: 4 3 2 1**

_____ **1.** Locate the horn(s) and describe their location. ______________________

____

_____ **2.** One horn or two? ______________

_____ **3.** What is the color of the wire to the horn(s)? ______________________

_____ **4.** Locate the horn relay and describe its location. ______________________

_____ **5.** The colors of the wires on the relay include: ____________, ____________,

____________, ____________, ____________

_____ **6.** Check the service information and compare the wire colors with the wiring schematic.

Agree? Yes ___ No ___ If no, what is the difference? ______________

_____ **6.** List the diagnostic procedure steps if the horn is inoperable.

1. ______________ 6. ______________
2. ______________ 7. ______________
3. ______________ 8. ______________
4. ______________ 9. ______________
5. ______________ 10. ______________

_____ **7.** What is the necessary action? ______________

____

____

____

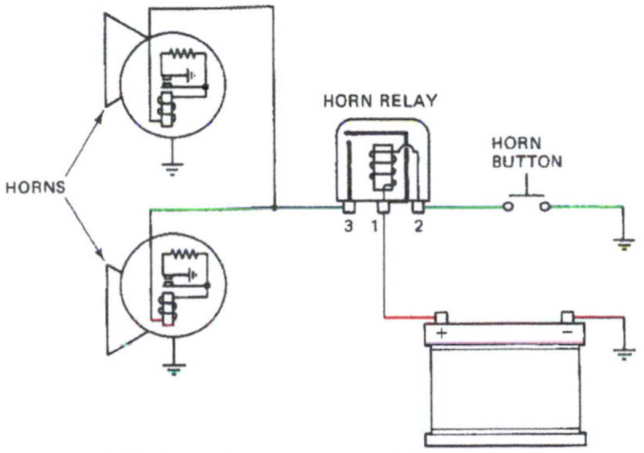
HORN RELAY
HORN BUTTON
HORNS
3
1
2
+
−

We Support NATEF

Windshield Wiper/Washer

Meets NATEF Task: (A6-G-2 and A6-G-3) Diagnose incorrect wiper operation; perform necessary action. (P-2)

Name ______________________________ **Date** __________ **Time on Task** _________

Make/Model ________________________ **Year** _________ **Evaluation: 4 3 2 1**

_____ **1.** Check service information for the specified testing procedure for a fault with the windshield wiper or washer____

____

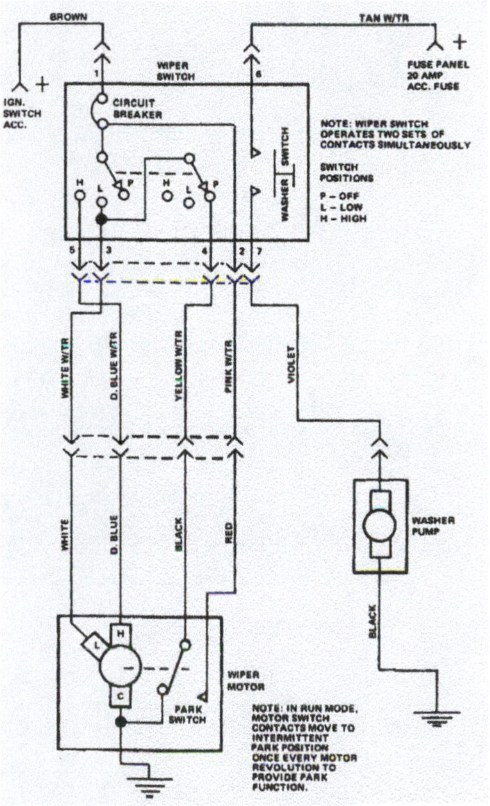

BROWN
TAN W/TR
+
FUSE PANEL
20 AMP
ACC. FUSE
WIPER
SWITCH
1
6
+
IGN.
SWITCH
ACC.
CIRCUIT
BREAKER
NOTE: WIPER SWITCH
OPERATES TWO SETS OF
CONTACTS SIMULTANEOUSLY
SWITCH
POSITIONS
P – OFF
L – LOW
H – HIGH
WASHER SWITCH
H L P H L P
5 3 4 2 7
WHITE W/TR
D. BLUE W/TR
YELLOW W/TR
PINK W/TR
VIOLET
WHITE
D. BLUE
BLACK
RED
WASHER
PUMP
BLACK
H
L
C
WIPER
MOTOR
PARK
SWITCH
NOTE: IN RUN MODE,
MOTOR SWITCH
CONTACTS MOVE TO
INTERMITTENT
PARK POSITION
ONCE EVERY MOTOR
REVOLUTION TO
PROVIDE PARK
FUNCTION.

_____ **2.** Operate the windshield wipers on all speeds.

OK _____ **NOT OK** _____

_____ **3.** Locate the windshield wiper/washer and describe their locations: ______________________________

____

_____ **4.** List the wire colors that are attached to the windshield wiper/washer motor assembly.

Wiper	**Washer**
a. ______________	a. ______________
b. ______________	b. ______________
c. ______________	c. ______________

_____ **5.** Based on the specified test results, what is the necessary action? _______________

____

Blower Motor Circuit

Meets NATEF Task: (A6-H-1) Diagnose operation of motor-driven accessory; determine necessary action. (P-2)

Name ______________________ **Date** __________ **Time on Task** __________

Make/Model ______________________ **Year** __________ **Evaluation: 4 3 2 1**

_____ **1.** Check service information and determine the specified testing procedures.

____

____

_____ **2.** Locate the blower motor schematic and determine the following information:

a. Describe the location ______________________

b. Is the blower motor accessible from inside the vehicle or from under the hood?

____

c. List the wire colors and their gauge:

Power = ______________

Ground = ______________

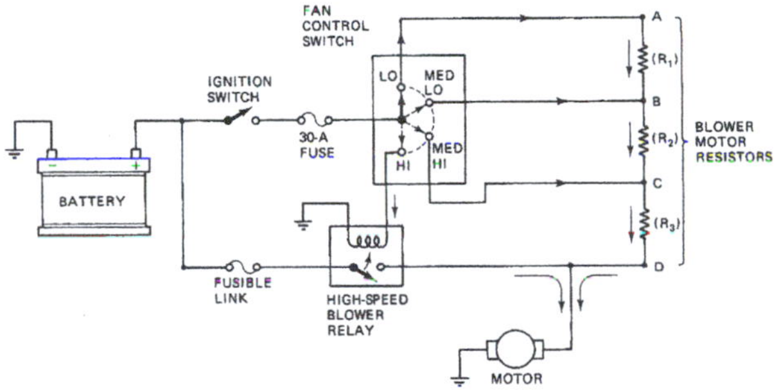

FAN CONTROL SWITCH
IGNITION SWITCH
LO
MED LO
MED HI
HI
30-A FUSE
BATTERY
FUSIBLE LINK
HIGH-SPEED BLOWER RELAY
A
B
C
D
(R1)
(R2)
(R3)
BLOWER MOTOR RESISTORS
MOTOR

_____ **3.** How are the various speeds controlled?

_____ Resistor pack

_____ Electronic controller

_____ Other (describe) ______________________

_____ **4.** What fuse number (label) and amperage rating are used for the blower motor?

a. Fuse number (label) ______________________

b. Fuse rating ______________________

_____ **5.** Describe the location of the ground(s) for the blower motor circuit. ______________

____

_____ **6.** Measure the current draw of the blower motor on high speed.

Amperage = __________ (normal blower motor amperage draw is about 12-14 amperes)

_____ **7.** Based on the inspection and test results, what is the necessary action? ___________

____

Power Accessory Diagnosis

Meets NATEF Task: (A6-H-1, A6-H-2, A6-H-3) Diagnose motor-driven accessory circuits; determine necessary action. (P-2, P-3, P-2)

Name ____________________ **Date** __________ **Time on Task** __________

Make/Model ____________________ **Year** __________ **Evaluation:** **4 3 2 1**

_____ **1.** Check service information for specified testing procedures to diagnose fault(s) in the power accessory systems.

____

____

_____ **2.** Locate the power window schematics and determine the following information.

a. Describe the location of the power window master control switch __________

____

b. Describe the location of the rear defogger relay ____________________

____

c. Describe the location of the cruise control servo unit (if equipped) __________

____

_____ **3.** Describe the specified testing procedure (major steps)

____

____

____

____

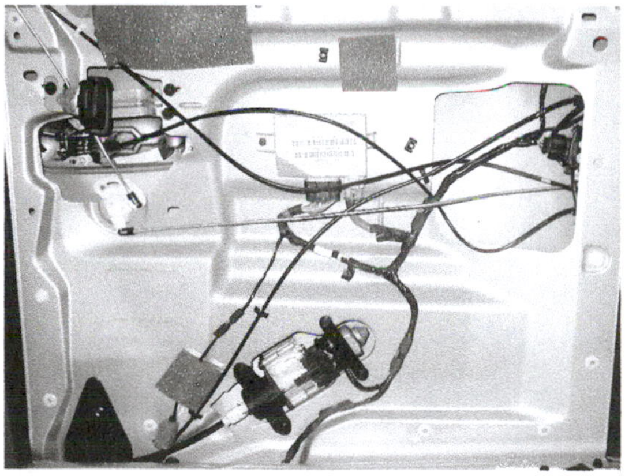

_____ **4.** Describe the ground(s) for the power windows.

____

____

_____ **5.** Based on the inspection and test results, what is the necessary action? __________

____

Door Panel

Meets NATEF Task: (A6-H-6) Remove and reinstall door panel. (P-1)

Name ______________________ **Date** __________ **Time on Task** __________

Make/Model ____________________ **Year** __________ **Evaluation: 4 3 2 1**

_____ **1.** Check service information for the specified procedures to follow to remove and reinstall a door panel. ____

____

_____ **2.** List the tools needed. ____

_____ **3.** Show the instructor the removed door panel. **Instructor's OK** __________

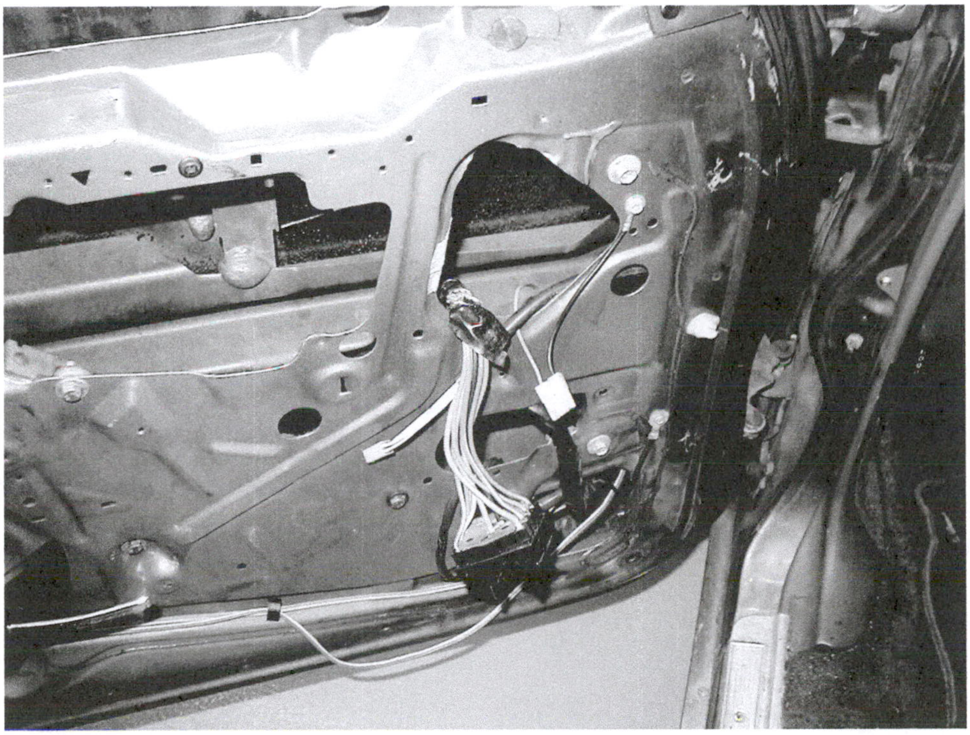

_____ **4.** How many clips and fasteners hold the door panel? ______________________

_____ **5.** Show the instructor the reinstalled door panel. **Instructor's OK** __________

Body and Module Communication Diagnosis

Meets NATEF Task: (A6-H-12) Diagnose body electronic system circuits using a scan tool. (P-2)

Name ______________________ **Date** __________ **Time on Task** __________

Make/Model ______________________ **Year** __________ **Evaluation: 4 3 2 1**

_____ **1.** Check service information for the procedures to follow for diagnosing body electronic system diagnosis using a scan tool.

____

____

_____ **2.** Check all that apply:

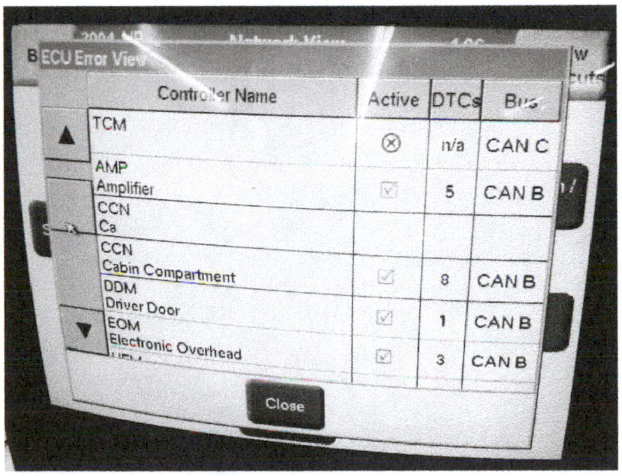
ECU Error View
Controller Name
Active
DTCs
Bus
TCM
n/a
CAN C
AMP
Amplifier
5
CAN B
CCN
Ca
CCN
Cabin Compartment
8
CAN B
DDM
Driver Door
1
CAN B
EOM
Electronic Overhead
3
CAN B
Close

___ Use a factory scan tool.

___ Use a global OBD-II scan tool.

___ Use a DMM to check for resistance on communication circuits.

___ Use a fused jumper wire and a scan tool to diagnose communication errors.

___ Other (describe) ____

_____ **3.** List the systems or components that can be accessed using a scan tool.

a. ______________________ f. ______________________

b. ______________________ g. ______________________

c. ______________________ h. ______________________

d. ______________________ j. ______________________

e. ______________________ k. ______________________

other (specify) ____

_____ **4.** List components or modules that can communicate with the scan tool. ______________

____

Keyless Entry and Anti-Theft Diagnosis

Meets NATEF Task: (A6-H-2) Diagnose problems with the anti-theft system. (P-2)

Name ______________________ **Date** __________ **Time on Task** __________

Make/Model ______________________ **Year** __________ **Evaluation: 4 3 2 1**

_____ **1.** Check service information for the specified testing procedures for the anti-theft system. ______________________________

____

_____ **2.** List the tools and/or equipment needed or specified.

a. ______________________

b. ______________________

c. ______________________

d. ______________________

e. ______________________

f. ______________________

_____ **3.** Describe the root cause of the fault(s) and action needed to restore proper operation of the anti-theft system.

____

____

____

_____ **4.** Perform any needed software updates or reprogramming.

____

____

____

We Support NATEF

Airbag Diagnosis

Meets NATEF Task: (A6-H-4) Diagnose supplemental restraint systems; determine necessary action. (P-2)

Name ______________________ **Date** __________ **Time on Task** __________

Make/Model ______________________ **Year** __________ **Evaluation: 4 3 2 1**

_____ **1.** Check service information for specified diagnostic test procedures. ____________

____

_____ **2.** Locate the airbag schematic and determine the following information.

a. Describe the location of the airbag controller ______________________

____

b. Describe the location of the arming sensor ______________________

____

c. Describe the location of the discriminating sensors ______________________

____

_____ **3.** What fuse number (label) and amperage rating is used for the airbag?

a. Fuse number (label) __________

b. Fuse rating ______________

_____ **4.** Describe the location of the ground(s) for the airbag. ______________

____

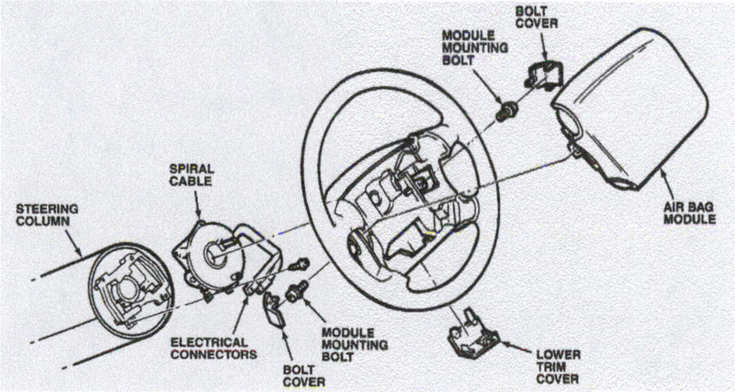
BOLT COVER
MODULE MOUNTING BOLT
SPIRAL CABLE
STEERING COLUMN
AIR BAG MODULE
ELECTRICAL CONNECTORS
MODULE MOUNTING BOLT
BOLT COVER
LOWER TRIM COVER

_____ **5.** Based on the diagnostic tests, what is the necessary action? ______________

____

____

Disarm and Enable Airbags

Meets NATEF Task: (A6-H-5) Disarm and enable the airbag system for vehicle service. (P-1)

Name ______________________ **Date** __________ **Time on Task** __________

Make/Model ______________________ **Year** __________ **Evaluation: 4 3 2 1**

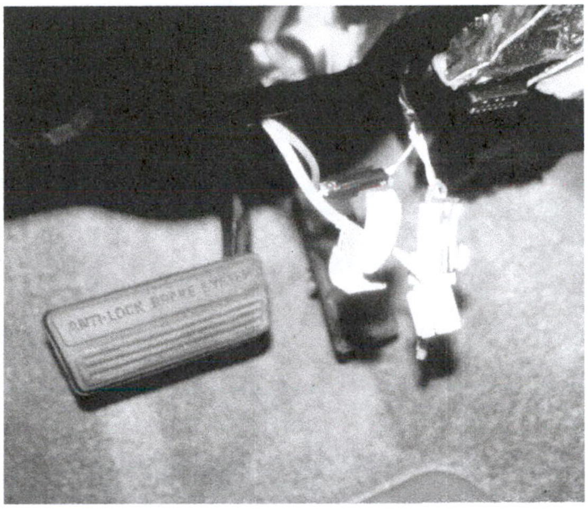
ANTI-LOCK BRAKE SYSTEM

Airbags should be temporarily disabled whenever working on or around the steering column or dash areas of a vehicle equipped with airbags.

_____ **1.** Check service information for the specified method to use to disarm and enable the airbags.

____

____

____

_____ **2.** Disconnect the negative (-) battery cable.

_____ **3.** Locate and remove the airbag fuse.

Label of fuse = ______________________

Amperage rating of the fuse = __________

_____ **4.** Remove the covering from underneath the steering column to gain access to the steering column airbag wiring connector.

_____ **5.** Disconnect the yellow airbag electrical connector.

_____ **6.** Locate and disconnect the yellow passenger side airbag electrical connector.

Describe the location ______________________________

What components had to be removed to gain access to the passenger side airbag connector? ______________________________

_____ **7.** After servicing the steering column or dash, restore the airbags by reconnecting the connectors, installing the airbag circuit fuse, and reconnecting the battery.

_____ **8.** Start the engine and check for proper operation of the airbag warning light.

OK _____ **NOT OK** _____

Radio Diagnosis

Meets NATEF Task: (A6-H-11) Diagnose radio static and weak or no reception; determine necessary action. (P-3)

Name ______________________ **Date** __________ **Time on Task** __________

Make/Model ______________________ **Year** __________ **Evaluation: 4 3 2 1**

_____ **1.** Check service information for the specified diagnostic procedures to locate and correct reception concerns. ____

____

_____ **2.** Locate the audio system schematic and determine the following information.

a. Fuse number (or name) and the rating of the fuse to the radio or receiver.

Fuse identification _______________ Rating _______________

b. Type and location of the antenna(s). Check all that apply.

_____ Front windshield _____ Rear Window

_____ Mast (front) _____ Other (describe) __________

_____ Mast (rear) ______________________

c. Check the components used in the system.

_____ Receiver _____ Separate CD/cassette player

_____ Separate amplifier _____ Integrated CD/cassette

_____ Equalizer _____ Amplified speakers

_____ Other (describe) ______________________________________

_____ **3.** Describe the location of the ground(s) for the audio system. ______________

____

_____ **4.** Based on the diagnostic procedures, what is the necessary action? ___________

____

____

We Support NATEF

OBD II Connector Identification

Meets NATEF Task: (A8-A-2) Locate and interpret vehicle and major component identification numbers. (P-1)

Name ______________________ **Date** __________ **Time on Task** __________

Make/Model ______________________ **Year** __________ **Evaluation: 4 3 2 1**

_____ **1.** Check service information and check which cavities of the OBD II diagnostic link connector (DLC) have electrical (metal) terminals.

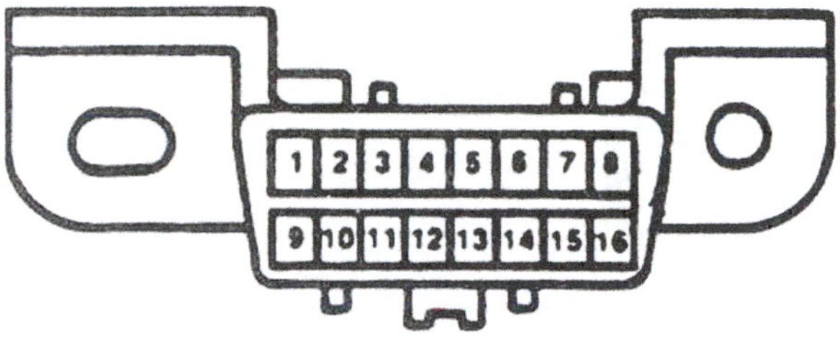
1
2
3
4
5
6
7
8
9
10
11
12
13
14
15
16

_____ **2.** Use service information and determine the identification for each of the terminals.

1. ______________________
2. ______________________
3. ______________________
4. ______________________
5. ______________________
6. ______________________
7. ______________________
8. ______________________
9. ______________________
10. ______________________
11. ______________________
12. ______________________
13. ______________________
14. ______________________
15. ______________________
16. ______________________

Retrieving OBD II Diagnostic Trouble Codes

Meets NATEF Task: (A8-B-5) Diagnose the causes of emissions or driveability concerns with stored or active diagnostic trouble codes; obtain, graph, and interpret scan tool data. (P-1)

Name ______________________ **Date** __________ **Time on Task** __________

Make/Model ______________________ **Year** __________ **Evaluation: 4 3 2 1**

A scan tool is required to retrieve diagnostic trouble codes from an OBD II vehicle. Every OBD II scan tool will be able to read all generic **Society of Automotive Engineers (SAE)** DTCs from any vehicle.

_____ **1.** Retrieve the DTCs using a scan tool.

(Specify which scan tool was used = _______________.)

__________ __________ __________ __________ __________

_____ **2.** If no DTCs are displayed, set a DTC by disconnecting a sensor such as the throttle position (TP) sensor and then starting and running the engine.

_____ **3.** Did the scan tool display both a generic OBD II (Poxxx) code *and* a manufacturer's specific DTC (P1xxx) code?

Yes ____ **No** ____

_____ **4.** Clear the stored DTCs using the scan tool.

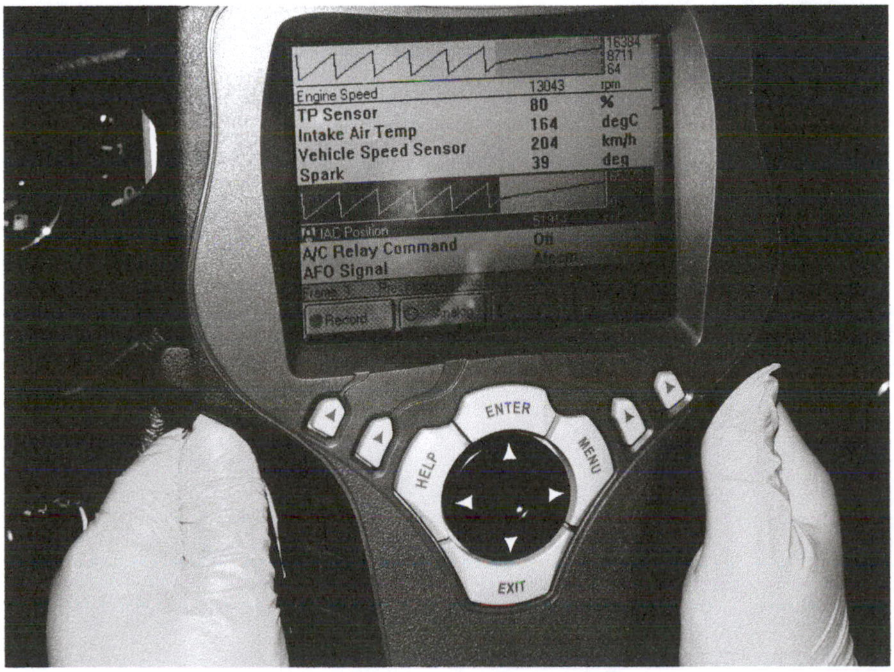
Engine Speed
TP Sensor
Intake Air Temp
Vehicle Speed Sensor
Spark
13043
80
164
204
39
rpm
%
degC
km/h
deg
IAC Position
A/C Relay Command
AFO Signal
Record
ENTER
MENU
HELP
EXIT

OBD II Monitors Status

Meets NATEF Task: (A8-B-1 and A8-B-4) Describe the importance of running all OBDII monitors for repair verification. (P-1)

Name ______________________ **Date** __________ **Time on Task** __________

Make/Model ______________________ **Year** __________ **Evaluation:** 4 3 2 1

_____ **1.** Check service information for the specified procedures and test equipment needed to determine the status of the inspection and maintenance (I/M) monitors.

____

____

_____ **2.** Connect a scan tool and check the status of the I/M monitors and list their status.

Monitor	**Status**
______________	______________
______________	______________
______________	______________
______________	______________
______________	______________

_____ **3.** Check service information and determine under what condition the vehicle must be driven to have the monitors run.

____

_____ **4.** Based on the results, what is the necessary action? ______________________

____

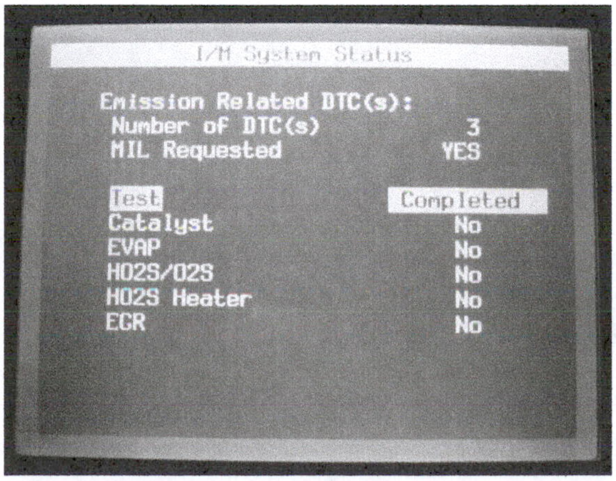
I/M System Status
Emission Related DTC(s):
Number of DTC(s) 3
MIL Requested YES
Test Completed
Catalyst No
EVAP No
HO2S/O2S No
HO2S Heater No
EGR No

We Support NATEF

Temperature Sensor Scan Tool Diagnosis

Meets NATEF Task: (A8-B-7) Inspect and test sensors, actuators, and circuits using a graphing multimeter (GMM)/digital storage oscilloscope (DSO); perform necessary action. (P-1)

Name ______________________ **Date** __________ **Time on Task** __________

Make/Model ______________________ **Year** __________ **Evaluation: 4 3 2 1**

_____ **1.** Check service information for the recommended method for checking temperature sensors using a scan tool.

____

____

_____ **2.** List all of the temperature sensors that are on the vehicle. Check all that apply.

_____ ECT (describe location) ______________________

_____ IAT (describe location) ______________________

_____ TFT (describe location) ______________________

_____ Other (describe) ______________________

_____ **3.** On a vehicle that has not been operated for several hours, use a scan tool and list the temperature displayed for various temperature sensors.

ECT = _______

IAT = _______

TFT = _______

Other (describe) = ______________________

____

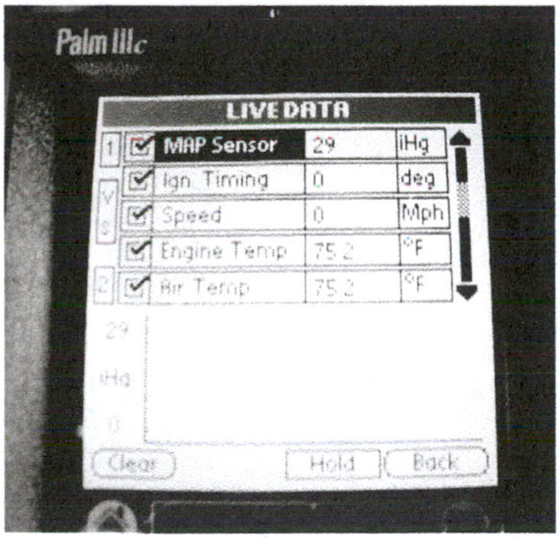
Palm IIIc
LIVE DATA
MAP Sensor 29 iHg
Ign Timing 0 deg
Speed 0 Mph
Engine Temp 75.2 °F
Air Temp 75.2 °F
Clear
Hold
Back

_____ **4.** Based on the test results, what is the necessary action? ______________________

____

Throttle Position Sensor Scope Test

Meets NATEF Task: (A8-B-7) Inspect and test sensors, actuators, and circuits using a graphing multimeter (GMM)/digital storage oscilloscope (DSO); perform necessary action. (P-1)

Name ______________________________ **Date** __________ **Time on Task** __________

Make/Model ________________________ **Year** __________ **Evaluation: 4 3 2 1**

_____ **1.** Check service information regarding the location of the throttle position sensor used on the vehicle being tested.

Location (describe):

____

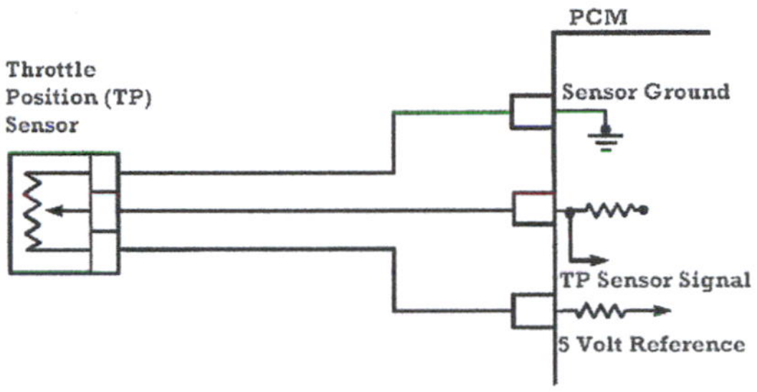
PCM
Throttle Position (TP) Sensor
Sensor Ground
TP Sensor Signal
5 Volt Reference

_____ **2.** Check service information for the wire colors used and their purpose

Wire 1 (color and purpose): ________________________

Wire 2 (color and purpose): ________________________

Wire 3 (color and purpose): ________________________

_____ **3.** Measure the reference voltage (should be close to 5 volts) = ________.

_____ **4.** Measure the sensor signal voltage at idle ____________,

specification = __________________.

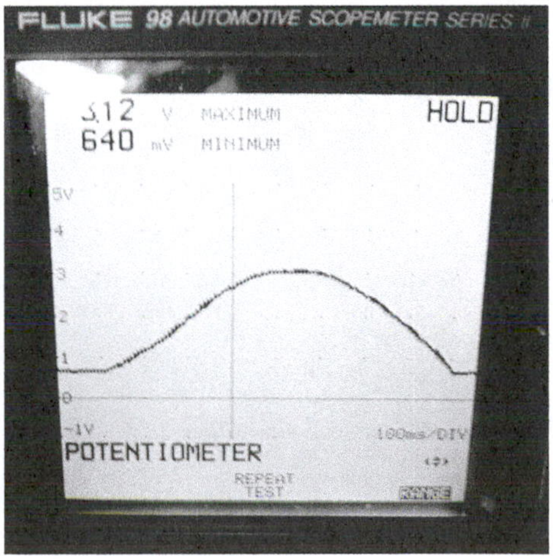
FLUKE 98 AUTOMOTIVE SCOPEMETER SERIES II
3.12 V MAXIMUM
640 mV MINIMUM
HOLD
5V
4
3
2
1
0
-1V
100ms/DIV
POTENTIOMETER
REPEAT TEST

_____ **5.** Measure the TP sensor at wide-open throttle (W.O.T.) = __________________ volts (should be about 4.5 volts).

_____ **6.** Following the test equipment manufacturer's instructions, show the instructor the waveform.

Instructor OK _______

_____ **7.** Based on the comparison between the captured waveform and the specified waveform, what action is needed?

____

MAP Sensor Diagnosis

Meets NATEF Task: (A8-B-7) Inspect and test sensors, actuators, and circuits using a graphing multimeter (GMM)/digital storage oscilloscope (DSO); perform necessary action. (P-1)

Name ______________________ **Date** __________ **Time on Task** __________

Make/Model ______________________ **Year** __________ **Evaluation: 4 3 2 1**

_____ **1.** Check service information for the specified MAP sensor diagnosis procedure.

____

_____ **2.** Perform a thorough visual inspection including:

a. Check the condition of vacuum hose (if equipped).
b. Check that the vacuum hose routing does not have any dips or sags in the vacuum hose between the sensor and the intake manifold.

NOTE: A dip or low portion in the vacuum hose can create a trap where liquid fuel (condensed gasoline fumes) or water (condensed steam) can accumulate and block the vacuum signal to the MAP sensor.

c. Disconnect the vacuum hose (if equipped) from the MAP sensor. If anything such as a liquid or other substance comes out of the sensor or the hose, replace the MAP sensor. Reconnect the vacuum hose to the MAP.

_____ **3.** Turn the ignition key on (engine off), read and record the MAP sensor voltage (or frequency) = _____ volts (Hz) (use either a scan tool or digital meter connected to the signal wire). (Should be about 4.60 to 4.80 volts or 156-159 Hz.)

OK _____ **NOT OK** _____

_____ **4.** Start the engine and operate until normal operating temperature is achieved. Read and record the MAP sensor voltage (or Hz) at idle speed = ________volts (Hz). (Should be between 0.9 and 1.6 volts (102-109 Hz) if the engine varies between 17 and 21 inches of Hg.) **OK** _____ **NOT OK** _____

_____ **5.** Based on these tests, what is the necessary action?

____

____

____

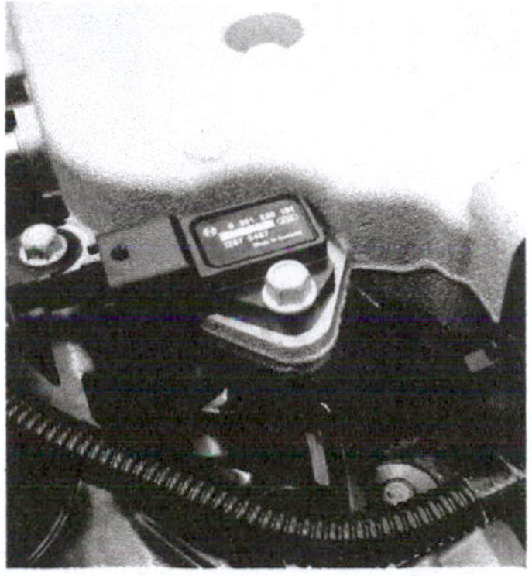

MAF Sensor Diagnosis

Meets NATEF Task: (A8-B-7) Inspect and test sensors, actuators, and circuits using a graphing multimeter (GMM)/digital storage oscilloscope (DSO); perform necessary action. (P-1)

Name ______________________ **Date** __________ **Time on Task** __________

Make/Model ______________________ **Year** __________ **Evaluation: 4 3 2 1**

A "*M*ass *A*ir *F*low" sensor produces a variable output depending on the MASS of the air flow through the sensor. A faulty MAF can cause driveability problems and stalling. A good MAF sensor should produce a signal that increases with engine speed.

_____ **1.** Check service information for the specified procedure to follow to test the MAF sensor.

____

_____ **2.** Use a meter or scope with a frequency counter to record frequency or voltage at idle and at WOT (short bursts).

at idle = ____________ at WOT = ____________

_____ **3.** Use a scan tool and record grams per second.

at idle = ____________ at WOT = ____________

A good MAF should read:

- greater than 100 grams per second (scan tool diagnosis)
- higher than 7000 Hertz (7 KHz) (digital MAF)
- higher than 4 volts (analog MAF)

_____ **4.** If the MAF sensor reading does not exceed these values, the sensing wire may be contaminated or the sensor itself is defective.

_____ **5.** Based on the test results, what is the necessary action? ____________________

____

____

We Support NATEF

Oxygen Sensor Diagnosis

Meets NATEF Task: (A8-B-7) Inspect and test sensors, actuators, and circuits using a graphing multimeter (GMM)/digital storage oscilloscope (DSO); perform necessary action. (P-1)

Name ______________________ **Date** __________ **Time on Task** __________

Make/Model ______________________ **Year** __________ **Evaluation: 4 3 2 1**

_____ **1.** Connect the scan tool to the DLC and start the engine.

TECH 2

_____ **2.** Operate the engine at a fast idle (2500 RPM) for 2 minutes to allow time for the oxygen sensor to warm to operating temperature.

_____ **3.** Observe the oxygen sensor activity on the scan tool to verify closed loop operation.

_____ **4.** Select "snap shot" mode and hold the engine speed steady and start recording.

_____ **5.** Play back snap shot and place a mark beside each range of oxygen sensor voltage for each frame of the snap shot.

Between 0 and 300 mV	**Between 300 and 600 mV**	**Between 600 and 1000 mV**
______________	______________	______________
(record # of times)	(record # of times)	(record # of times)

_____ **6.** Results: A good oxygen sensor and computer system should result in most snap shot values at both ends (0 to 300 and 600 to 1000 mV). If most of the readings are in the middle, the oxygen sensor is not working correctly.

OK _______ **NOT OK** _______

_____ **7.** Based on the test results, what is the necessary action? ______________________

____

We Support NATEF

Wide-Band Oxygen Sensor

Meets NATEF Task: (A8-B-7) Inspect and test sensors, actuators, and circuits using a graphing multimeter (GMM)/digital storage oscilloscope (DSO); perform necessary action. (P-1)

Name ______________________________ **Date** __________ **Time on Task** __________

Make/Model ________________________ **Year** _________ **Evaluation: 4 3 2 1**

_____ **1.** Wide-band oxygen sensors use four, five, or six wires. Check service information for the color and identification of each of the wires used on the wide-band oxygen sensors.

	Wire Color	Purpose	Typical Voltage on Wire During Closed-Loop Operation
a.	__________	______________________	__________
b.	__________	______________________	__________
c.	__________	______________________	__________
d.	__________	______________________	__________
e.	__________	______________________	__________
f.	__________	______________________	__________

_____ **2.** Check service information for the specified testing procedure for diagnosing the wide-band oxygen sensor.

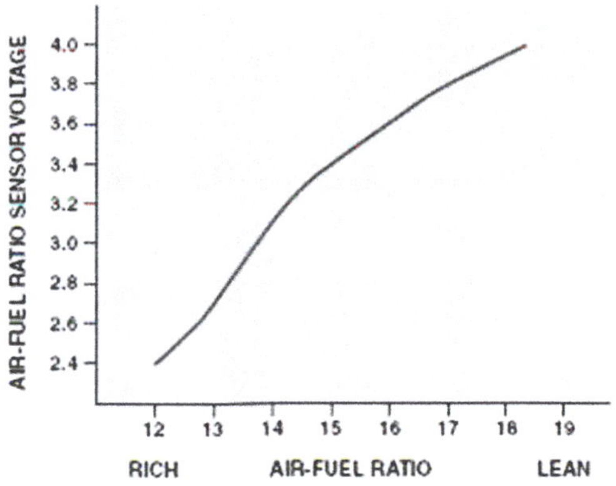
AIR-FUEL RATIO SENSOR VOLTAGE
4.0
3.8
3.6
3.4
3.2
3.0
2.8
2.6
2.4
12
13
14
15
16
17
18
19
RICH
AIR-FUEL RATIO
LEAN

____

____

Check all that are specified:

____ Scan tool
____ DMM
____ DSO
____ Other (describe) ______________________________

_____ **3.** Based on the results of the specified test procedure, what is the necessary action?

____

____

Ignition System Identification

Meets NATEF Task: (A8-A-2) Research applicable vehicle and service information, such as engine management system operation, vehicle service history, service precautions, and TSBs. (P-1)

Name ______________________ **Date** __________ **Time on Task** __________

Make/Model ______________________ **Year** __________ **Evaluation: 4 3 2 1**

_____ **1.** Check service information and determine what type of ignition system is used on this vehicle?

_____ Distributor ignition (DI)
_____ Waste-spark (EI)
_____ Coil-on-plug
_____ Other (describe)
____
____

DO NOT REMOVE SPARK PLUGS WHEN HOT
FIRING
ORDER

_____ **2.** Check service information and determine what type of primary circuit switching device is used on this system.

_____ Pickup coil (pulse generator) Used on most distributor-type ignition systems.
_____ Hall-effect sensor
_____ Magnetic sensor
_____ Optical sensor
_____ Other (describe) ______________________

_____ **3.** What color wires are used on the switching device?

__________, __________, __________, __________

_____ **4.** Using service information, determine where the primary ignition switching device signal goes:

_____ Ignition control module (ICM)
_____ Computer (PCM)
_____ Other (describe) ______________________

Electronic Ignition Diagnosis

Meets NATEF Task: (A8-C-1) Diagnose electronic ignition-related problems; determine necessary action. (P-1)

Name ______________________ **Date** __________ **Time on Task** __________

Make/Model ______________________ **Year** __________ **Evaluation: 4 3 2 1**

_____ **1.** Check service information for the specified diagnostic procedures to follow when troubleshooting the ignition system.

____

____

____

_____ **2.** Most test procedures specify that the spark be tested using a spark tester. Use a spark tester and determine that a spark does occur at each cylinder.

Cylinder #1 ______ **OK** ____ **NOT OK** ____ (describe) ______________

Cylinder #2 ______ **OK** ____ **NOT OK** ____ (describe) ______________

Cylinder #3 ______ **OK** ____ **NOT OK** ____ (describe) ______________

Cylinder #4 ______ **OK** ____ **NOT OK** ____ (describe) ______________

Cylinder #5 ______ **OK** ____ **NOT OK** ____ (describe) ______________

Cylinder #6 ______ **OK** ____ **NOT OK** ____ (describe) ______________

Cylinder #7 ______ **OK** ____ **NOT OK** ____ (describe) ______________

Cylinder #8 ______ **OK** ____ **NOT OK** ____ (describe) ______________

_____ **3.** Based on the test results, what is the necessary action?

____

____

____

____

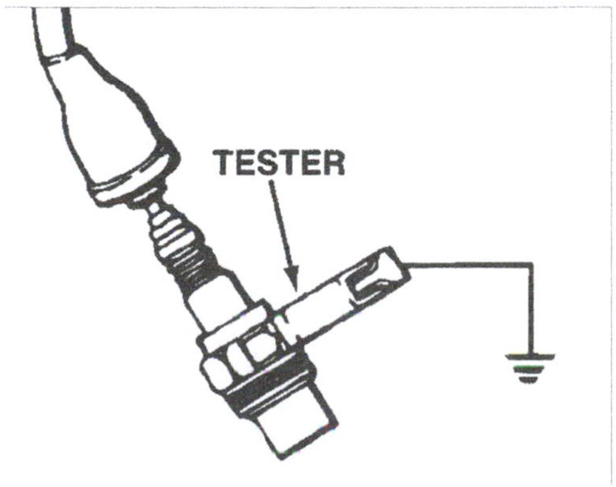
TESTER

We Support ASE NATEF

Ignition Scope Analysis

Meets NATEF Task: (A8-C-1) Inspect and test ignition primary and secondary circuit wiring and solid state components; test ignition coil(s); perform necessary action. (P-1)

Name ______________________ **Date** __________ **Time on Task** __________

Make/Model ______________________ **Year** __________ **Evaluation: 4 3 2 1**

_____ **1.** Check service information regarding the specified method for attaching and using a secondary circuit oscilloscope.

____

____

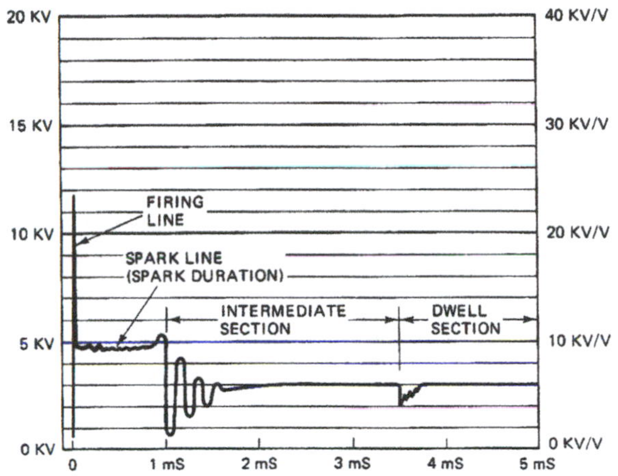

20 KV
15 KV
10 KV
5 KV
0 KV
40 KV/V
30 KV/V
20 KV/V
10 KV/V
0 KV/V
FIRING LINE
SPARK LINE (SPARK DURATION)
INTERMEDIATE SECTION
DWELL SECTION
0
1 mS
2 mS
3 mS
4 mS
5 mS

_____ **2.** Type of ignition:

_____ Distributor
_____ Waste spark
_____ Coil-on-plug

_____ **3.** Connect the ignition scope to the system as per the scope manufacturer's instructions.

_____ **4.** Brand of scope used: ______________________________

_____ **5.** Describe the hookup procedure. ______________________________

_____ **6.** Start the engine and observe the secondary ignition waveform.

	Firing Voltage (KV) (voltage should be 5-15 KV)	**Spark Line Length (ms)** (length should be 1-2 ms)
Cylinder #1	__________	__________
Cylinder #2	__________	__________
Cylinder #3	__________	__________
Cylinder #4	__________	__________
Cylinder #5	__________	__________
Cylinder #6	__________	__________
Cylinder #7	__________	__________
Cylinder #8	__________	__________

_____ 7. Based on the test results, what is the necessary action? ______________________________

Ignition Inspection and Testing

Meets NATEF Task: (A8-C-1) Inspect and test ignition primary and secondary circuit wiring and solid state components; test ignition coil(s); perform necessary action. (P-1)

Name ______________________ **Date** __________ **Time on Task** __________

Make/Model ______________________ **Year** __________ **Evaluation: 4 3 2 1**

_____ **1.** Check service information for the specifications and testing procedures for the secondary ignition wiring.

____

_____ **2.** Carefully check the spark plug wire for damage or burned areas that could indicate a break in the insulation.

OK _____ **NOT OK** _____

_____ **3.** Set the digital multimeter to read ohms (Ω).

_____ **4.** List the length in feet and the resistance values in ohms for each spark plug wire according to the cylinder number:

	Length (feet)	**Ohms**
1.	________	________
2.	________	________
3.	________	________
4.	________	________
5.	________	________
6.	________	________
7.	________	________
8.	________	________

Coil wire: (if equipped)

________ ________

_____ **5.** Results - Original equipment radio suppression wires should test 10,000 ohms (10KΩ) or *less* per foot of length.

OK _____ **NOT OK** _____

_____ **6.** Based on the inspection and test(s), what is the necessary action? ________________

____

We Support NATEF

Spark Plugs Inspection

Meets NATEF Task: (A8-C-4) Inspect and test ignition primary and secondary circuit wiring and solid state components; test ignition coil(s); perform necessary action. (P-1)

Name ____________________ **Date** __________ **Time on Task** __________

Make/Model ____________________ **Year** __________ **Evaluation: 4 3 2 1**

_____ **1.** Check service information and determine the correct plug code and gap for your vehicle using a spark plug application guide.

Engine: # Cylinders_____ VIN# ______________

Brand __________ Code # __________ Gap __________

_____ **2.** Remove and label all the spark plug wires.

_____ **3.** Determine the condition and gap of all spark plugs:

	Condition	**Gap**
1.	______________________	_______
2.	______________________	_______
3.	______________________	_______
4.	______________________	_______
5.	______________________	_______
6.	______________________	_______
7.	______________________	_______
8.	______________________	_______

_____ **4.** Reinstall the spark plug (start by hand).

_____ **5.** Use a torque wrench and torque the spark plugs to the proper torque.

Specified torque = ______________

_____ **6.** Start the engine. Check for possible rough running caused by crossed or loose spark plug wires.

OK _____ **NOT OK** _____

_____ **7.** Based on the inspection of the spark plugs, what is the necessary action? __________

____

Ignition Coil Testing

Meets NATEF Task: (A8-C-4) Inspect and test ignition primary and secondary circuit wiring and solid state components; test ignition coil(s); perform necessary action. (P-1)

Name ______________________________ **Date** __________ **Time on Task** __________

Make/Model ________________________ **Year** _________ **Evaluation:** 4 3 2 1

_____ **1.** Check service information for the specified ignition coil testing procedure.

____

_____ **2.** Visually inspect the coil(s) for carbon track and other faults. **OK** ___ **NOT OK** ___

_____ **3.** Check the primary winding resistance.

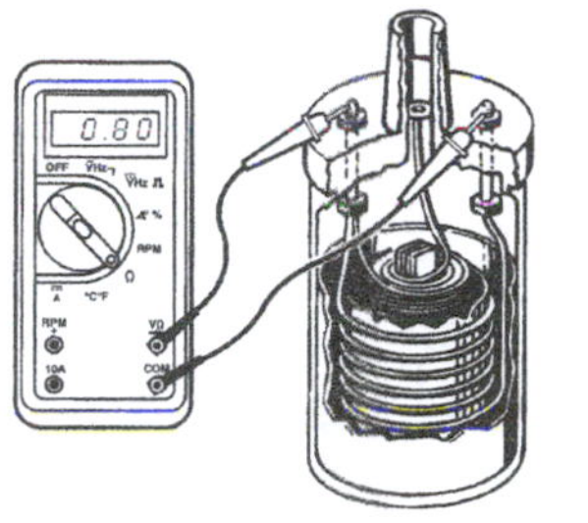
0.80

Specification: ______________________

Actual: __________________________

OK ____ **NOT OK** ____

_____ **4.** Check the secondary winding resistance.

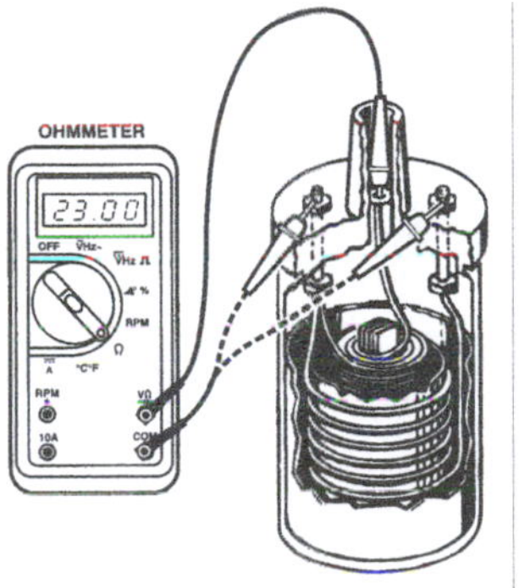
OHMMETER
23.00

Specification: ______________________

Actual: __________________________

OK ____ **NOT OK** ____

_____ **5.** Perform resistance checks for short-to-ground.

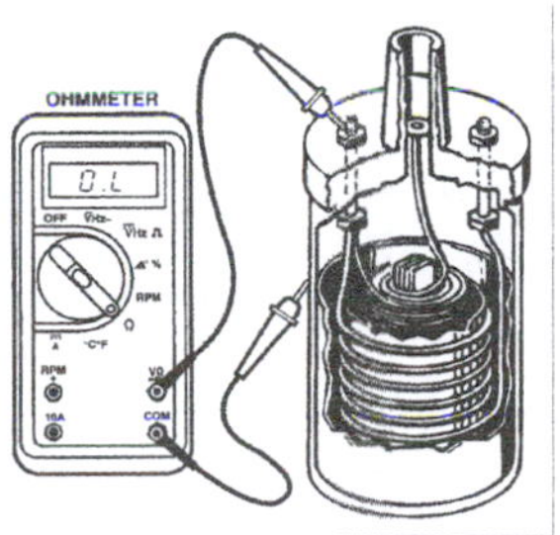
OHMMETER
0.L

OK ____ **NOT OK** ____

_____ **6.** Based on the inspection and tests, what is the necessary action? ________________

____

We Support ASE NATEF

Primary Ignition Inspection and Testing

Meets NATEF Task: (A8-C-2) Inspect, test, and/or replace ignition control module, powertrain/engine control module; reprogram as necessary. (P-2)

Name ______________________ **Date** __________ **Time on Task** __________

Make/Model ______________________ **Year** __________ **Evaluation: 4 3 2 1**

_____ **1.** Check service information and determine what type of ignition system is used on this vehicle?

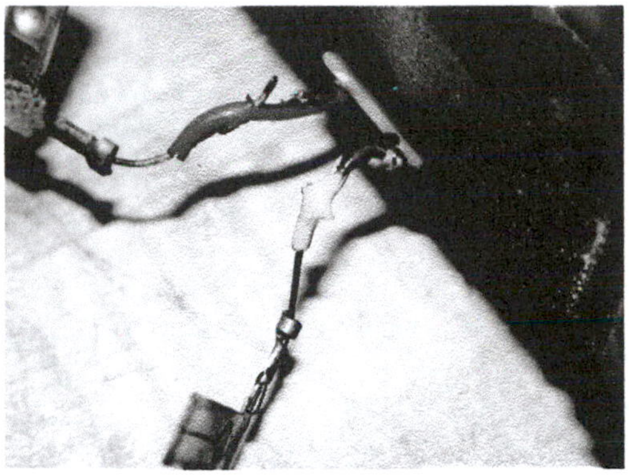

_____ Distributor ignition (DI)
_____ Waste-spark (EI)
_____ Coil-on-plug
_____ Other (describe) ______________________

_____ **2.** Check service information and determine what type of primary circuit switching device is used on this system.

_____ Pickup coil (pulse generator) Used on most distributor-type ignition systems.
_____ Hall-effect sensor
_____ Magnetic sensor
_____ Optical sensor
_____ Other (describe) ______________________

_____ **3.** Check service information and determine what color wires are used on the switching device?

______________, ______________, ______________, ______________

_____ **4.** The primary ignition switching device signal goes to the:

_____ Ignition control module (ICM)
_____ Computer (PCM)
_____ Other (describe) ______________________

_____ **5.** Using the service information, what are the steps to diagnosis a no-spark condition?

____
____
____

_____ **6.** Could a fault in the primary ignition sensor cause a no-spark condition?

Yes _____ No _____

_____ **7.** Based on inspection and tests, what is the necessary action? ______________________

Fuel Pump Testing

Meets NATEF Task: (A8-D-3) Inspect and test fuel pumps and pump control systems for pressure, regulation, and volume; perform necessary action. (P-1)

Name ______________________ **Date** __________ **Time on Task** __________

Make/Model ______________________ **Year** __________ **Evaluation: 4 3 2 1**

_____ **1.** Check service information and determine the factory specifications for acceptable fuel pump pressure.

Fuel pump pressure specifications = ______________________

_____ **2.** Check service information, locate the fuel system pressure test valve or port, and describe its location.

____

_____ **3.** Connect a fuel pressure gauge to the fuel pressure Schrader valve.

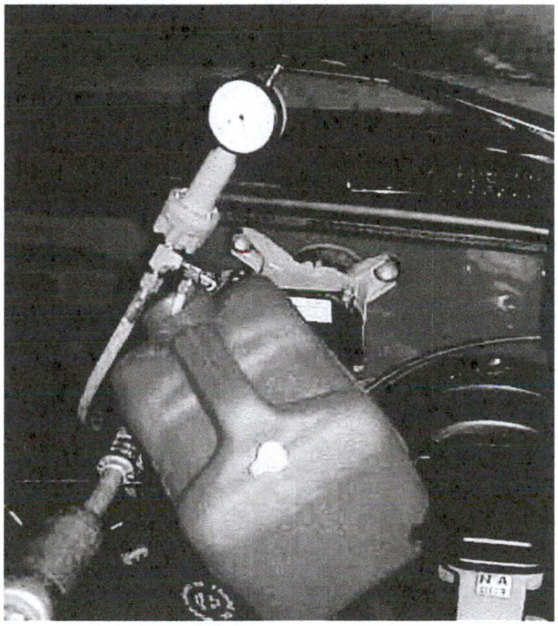

_____ **4.** Start the engine and observe the fuel pressure.

fuel pressure = ______________

OK _____ **NOT OK** _____

_____ **5.** Connect a hand-operated vacuum pump to the fuel pressure regulator and apply 20 in. Hg. of vacuum. Did the pressure decrease? __________

_____ **6.** Check fuel pump volume (0.5 to 1.0 gallons per minute).

_____ **7.** Based on this test, what is the necessary action?

____

____

____

Fuel Pump Current Draw Test

Meets NATEF Task: (A8-D-3) Inspect and test fuel pumps and pump control systems for pressure, regulation, and volume; perform necessary action. (P-1)

Name ______________________ **Date** __________ **Time on Task** __________

Make/Model ______________________ **Year** __________ **Evaluation: 4 3 2 1**

_____ **1.** Many electric fuel pumps can be measured for current draw in amperes. A higher than normal amperage draw may indicate a clogged fuel filter causing back pressure for the pump or a worn pump.

NOTE: Other makes and models of vehicles can be tested by connecting the ammeter in series with the fuel pump fuse and then operating the engine. Check the wiring diagram for your specific vehicle.

_____ **2.** Connect the digital multimeter, set to read amperes (A) and connect the red lead to the positive (+) of the battery. Connect the black lead to the fuel pump test terminal. The pump should run and an amperage reading should be observed on the meter. (Allow the pump to run for 30 seconds.) Confirm the reading with acceptable specifications.
Reading = ________ amp

Normal readings: TBI = 2 to 5 amps (9-13 psi)
Port injection = 4 to 8 amps (35-45 psi)
Central port injection = 8 to 12 amps (55-64 psi)

- If the current is *lower* than specifications, check for:

  1. poor electrical connection at the fuel pump relay.
  2. poor connection at the fuel pump electrical connector.
  3. poor ground connection.
  4. defective fuel pressure regulator

- If the current is *higher* than specifications, check for:

  1. clogged fuel filter.
  2. pinched fuel lines.
  3. slowly rotating fuel pump.

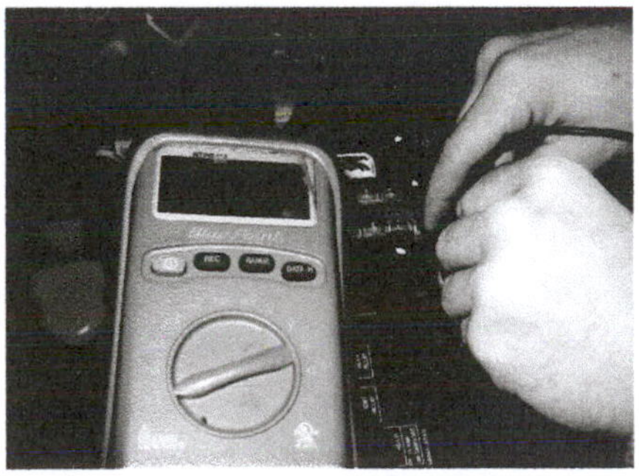

_____ **3.** Based on the test results, what is the necessary action?

____

____

Fuel Filter Replacement

Meets NATEF Task: (A8-D-4) Replace fuel filters. (P-2)

Name ______________________ **Date** __________ **Time on Task** __________

Make/Model ______________________ **Year** __________ **Evaluation: 4 3 2 1**

_____ **1.** Check service information for the recommended part number and fuel filter replacement procedure.

a. Fuel filter part number = ________________

b. Recommended procedure: ______________________________________

____

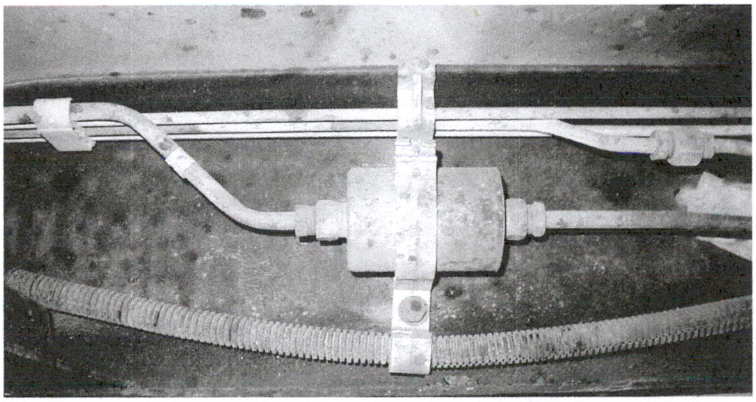

_____ **2.** Check all that apply:

____ Fuel system pressure should be relieved before removing the old filter

____ Special tools required to remove filter (describe): ____________________

____

____ Direction of fuel flow labeled on the filter? ____________________

____ Other (describe) ______________________________________

____

We Support NATEF

Air Intake Inspection

Meets NATEF Task: (A8-D-6) Perform active tests of actuators using a scan tool; determine necessary action. (P-1)

Name ______________________ **Date** __________ **Time on Task** __________

Make/Model ______________________ **Year** __________ **Evaluation: 4 3 2 1**

The idle air control is used to control idle speed by increasing or decreasing the amount of air entering the engine similar to what occurs when the accelerator pedal is depressed.

_____ **1.** Inspect throttle body and related components for vacuum leaks.

OK ____ **NOT OK** ____ Describe faults: ______________________

_____ **2.** Connect a scan tool.

_____ **3.** Look at the IAC commanded position = ________ (should be 15 to 25% or counts on a warm engine in park or neutral).

OK ____ **NOT OK** ____

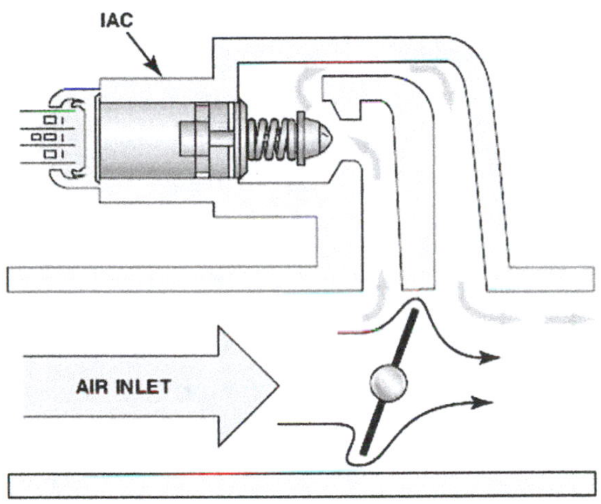
IAC
AIR INLET

Diagnosis:

- **IAC counts higher than normal.** This could indicate one or more of the following:
  1. Engine not fully warm
  2. Some electrical load is on, such as daytime running lights or air conditioning
  3. Dirty throttle plates
  4. Abnormal load on the engine
- **IAC counts lower than normal.** This could indicate one or more of the following:
  1. A vacuum leak
  2. Misadjusted idle speed control
  3. Stuck or binding throttle cable or linkage

_____ **3.** Based on the inspection of the system, what is the necessary action? ______________

____

We Support NATEF

Gasoline Direct Injection Identification

Meets NATEF Task: (A8-A-2) Research applicable vehicle and service information, such as engine management system operation, vehicle service history, and TSBs. (P-1)

Name ______________________ **Date** __________ **Time on Task** __________

Make/Model ______________________ **Year** __________ **Evaluation: 4 3 2 1**

_____ **1.** Check service information to determine if the vehicle being serviced is equipped with gasoline direct injection. (check all that apply)

____ Gasoline direct injection only

____ Port and gasoline direct injection system

_____ **2.** List the specifications as found in service information.

a. Lift pump pressure = ________

b. Lift pump volume = ________

c. High-pressure system pressure = _________

d. Fuel injector resistance = _________

e. Other (describe) ____

_____ **3.** What is the specified maintenance procedures required (if any)? Describe:

____

____

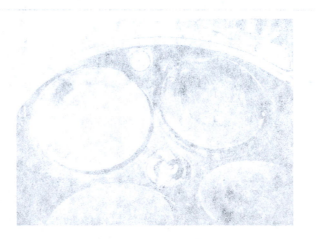

Electronic Throttle Control System ID

Meets NATEF Task: (A8-A-2) Research applicable vehicle and service information, such as engine management system operation, vehicle service history, and TSBs. (P-1)

Name ________________________ **Date** __________ **Time on Task** __________

Make/Model ________________________ **Year** __________ **Evaluation: 4 3 2 1**

_____ **1.** Check service information to determine if the vehicle being serviced is equipped with an electronic throttle control (ETC) system. Describe how it was determined. (check all that apply)

____ Visual inspection

____ Service information

____ Scan tool

____ Other (describe) ________________________________

_____ **2.** Does the electronic throttle control system use a cable between the accelerator pedal and the APP sensor?

____ Yes ____ No

_____ **3.** What is the relearn procedure that needs to be followed if the electronic throttle control system throttle body assembly is replaced? Describe the specified procedure.

____

____

____

Scan Tool Diagnosis

Meets NATEF Task: (A8-B-1) Retrieve and record diagnostic trouble codes, OBD monitor status, and freeze frame data; clear codes when applicable. (P-1)

Name ______________________________ **Date** __________ **Time on Task** __________

Make/Model ________________________ **Year** _________ **Evaluation: 4 3 2 1**

(Not all of this data will be available on all vehicles or scan tools - if not available, put NA.)

_____ **1.** DTCs: ________________ Pending DTC:________________________________

_____ **2.** Engine coolant temperature (ECT): cold _____ warm _______

_____ **3.** Intake air temperature (IAT): cold _____ warm ________

_____ **4.** Upstream O2S1: lowest voltage observed _____ highest voltage observed _____

_____ **5.** Upstream O2S2: lowest voltage observed _____ highest voltage observed _____

_____ **6.** Downstream O2S: lowest voltage observed _____ highest voltage observed _____

_____ **7.** O_2 cross counts: @ idle____ @ 2,000 RPM____

_____ **8.** Injector pulse width: @ idle (park)_____ @ idle (drive)_____
@ 2,000 RPM (park)_____ @ 3,000 RPM (park)_____

_____ **9.** Spark advance: @ idle (park)_____ @ idle (drive)_____
@ 2,000 RPM (park)_____ @ 3,000 RPM (park)_____

_____**10.** Short term fuel trim (integrator): @ idle (park)_____
@ idle (drive)_____ @ 2,000 RPM (park)_____

_____**11.** Long term fuel trim (block learn): @ idle (park)_____ @ idle (drive)_____

_____**12.** MAP: @ idle (park)_____ @ idle (drive)_____

_____**13.** MAF (grams/sec): @ idle (park)_____ @ idle (drive)_____
@ 2,000 RPM (park)_____ @ key on (engine off)_____

_____**14.** IAC counts: @ idle (park)_____ @ idle (drive)_____
@ A/C on (drive)_____ @ 2,000 RPM (park)_____

_____**15.** Throttle position (TP) sensor: @ idle____ @ W.O.T. engine off, ignition "on"_____

_____**16.** Battery voltage:__________

_____**17.** All monitors run and passed? OK_____ NOT OK_____

_____**18.** Troubles with the vehicle? (if any)________________________________

Fuel Trim Diagnosis

Meets NATEF Task: (A8-B-6) Diagnose emissions or driveability concerns without stored diagnostic trouble codes; determine necessary action. (P-1)

Name ______________________ **Date** __________ **Time on Task** __________

Make/Model ______________________ **Year** __________ **Evaluation:** 4 3 2 1

Fuel trim is the computer correction factor that uses the oxygen sensor to determine if more or less fuel needs to be delivered by the fuel injectors. Fuel trim is only available on a scan tool.

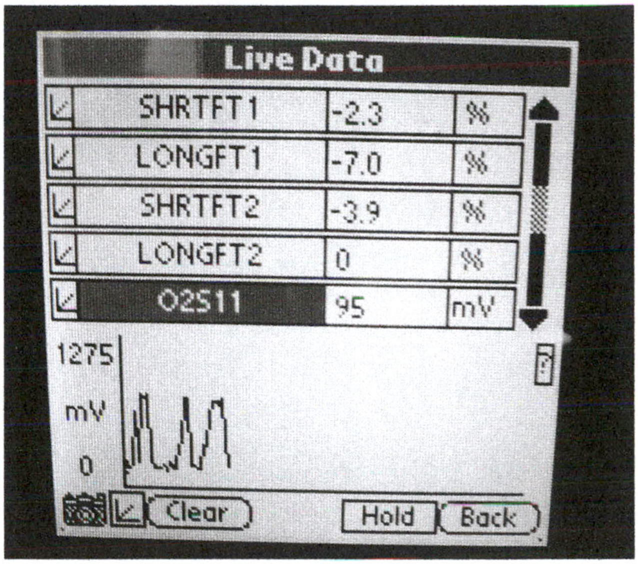
Live Data
SHRTFT1 -2.3 %
LONGFT1 -7.0 %
SHRTFT2 -3.9 %
LONGFT2 0 %
O2S11 95 mV
1275
mV
0
Clear
Hold
Back

_____ **1.** Connect a scan tool and select long-term fuel trim (LTFT) (block learn) and short-term fuel trim (STFT).

_____ **2.** Start the engine and operate until normal operating temperature and closed loop status is achieved.

_____ **3.** Record the following cell number and LTFT amount:

	Cell	LTFT	STFT
Idle in Drive (if automatic transmission only)	________	________	________
Idle in Park A/C off	________	________	________
Idle in Park A/C on	________	________	________
3000 RPM in Park	________	________	________

Results: Fuel trim should be within plus or minus 10% or within 118-138 if the block/integration is displayed as a binary number.

_____ **4.** Based on the test results, what is the necessary action? ______________________

____

Port Fuel-Injection System Diagnosis

Meets NATEF Task: (A8-D-1) Diagnose hot or cold no-starting, hard starting, poor driveability, incorrect idle speed, poor idle, flooding, hesitation, surging; determine necessary action. (P-1)

Name ______________________________ **Date** __________ **Time on Task** __________

Make/Model __________________________ **Year** __________ **Evaluation: 4 3 2 1**

_____ **1.** Check service information for the recommended procedure to follow to diagnose the fuel injection system.

_____ **2.** Attach a fuel pressure gauge to the Schrader valve on the fuel rail, if available.

_____ **3.** Turn the ignition key to "on" or start the engine to build up the fuel pump pressure.

_____psi (should reach specified fuel pressure, usually about 35-45 psi)

_____ **4.** Turn the ignition off and wait 20 minutes and observe the fuel pressure retained in the fuel rail = _______ psi. If the drop is less than 20 psi in 20 minutes, everything is OK. (The fuel pressure should *not* drop more than 20 psi in 20 minutes.)

If the drop is *greater* than 20 psi in 20 minutes, there is a possible problem with:

a. the check valve in the fuel pump.
b. leaking injectors.
c. a defective (leaking) fuel pressure regulator.

To determine which unit is defective, perform the following:

Step #1: Re-energize the electric fuel pump.

Step #2: Clamp the fuel *supply* line, wait 10 minutes. If the pressure drop does *not* occur - replace the fuel pump. If the pressure drop still occurs - continue with Step #3.

Step #3: Repeat the pressure build up of the electric pump and clamp the fuel return line. If the pressure drop time is now OK, replace the fuel pressure regulator.

Step #4: If the pressure drop still occurs, the injectors are leaking. Remove the injectors with the fuel rail and hold over paper. Replace those injectors that drip a drop or more after 10 minutes with pressurized fuel.

CAUTION: Do not clamp plastic fuel lines. Connect shut-off valves to the fuel system to shut off supply and return lines.

_____ **5.** Based on the test results, what is the necessary action? ______________________

Injector Resistance Testing

Meets NATEF Task: (A8-D-7) Inspect and test fuel injectors. (P-1)

Name ______________________________ **Date** __________ **Time on Task** __________

Make/Model ________________________ **Year** _________ **Evaluation:** **4 3 2 1**

_____ **1.** Check service information for the specified injector resistance. __________________

_____ **2.** Measure the resistance of all injectors with a digital ohmmeter.

NOTE: For best performance and idle quality, all injectors should measure within 0.3 to 0.4 ohms of each other.

Injector resistance:

Resistance	**Resistance**
1. __________	5. __________
2. __________	6. __________
3. __________	7. __________
4. __________	8. __________

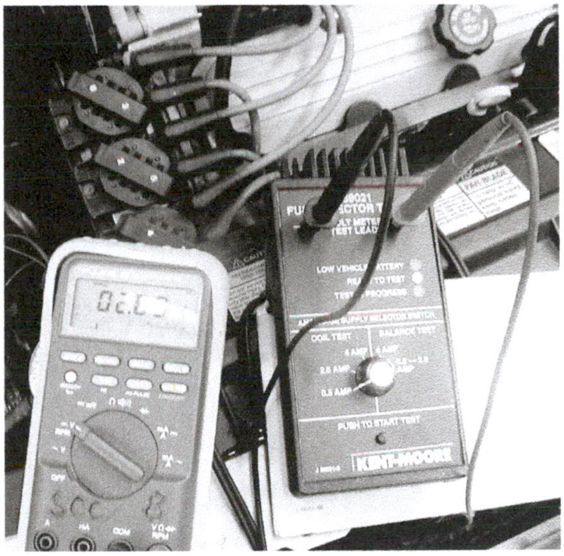
KENT-MOORE
PUSH TO START TEST

Highest resistance = ____ ohms.

Lowest resistance = ____ ohms.

Difference = ____ ohms (should be less than 0.4 ohms).

OK_____ **NOT OK**_____

Fuel Injector Balance Test

Meets NATEF Task: (A8-D-7) Inspect and test fuel injectors. (P-1)

Name ______________________ **Date** __________ **Time on Task** __________

Make/Model ______________________ **Year** __________ **Evaluation:** 4 3 2 1

_____ **1.** Check service information for the procedures and specifications for an injector voltage drop test.

____

____

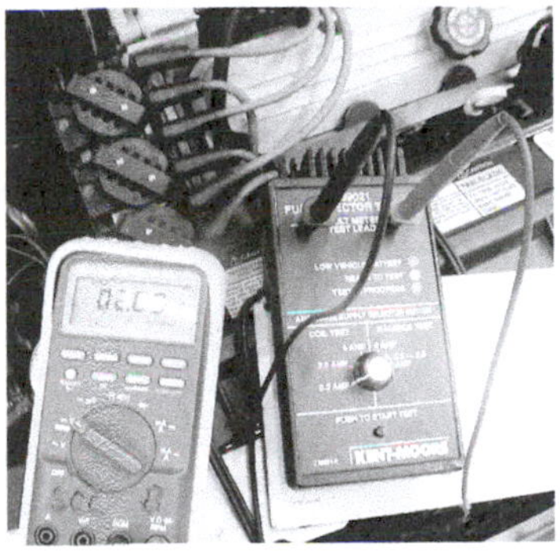

a. Part number of recommended tester = __________

b. Maximum allowable variation in voltage drop among the injectors = __________

_____ **2.** What was the starting pressure?

_________ psi/kPa

_____ **3.** Record the voltage drop of the injectors (pressure after injector was pulsed on).

Cylinder #1 __________ Cylinder #5 __________

Cylinder #2 __________ Cylinder #6 __________

Cylinder #3 __________ Cylinder #7 __________

Cylinder #4 __________ Cylinder #8 __________

_____ **4.** Compare the test results with the specifications. What is the necessary action?

____

____

Injector Voltage Waveform Test

Meets NATEF Task: (A8-D-7) Inspect and test fuel injectors. (P-1)

Name ______________________________ **Date** __________ **Time on Task** __________

Make/Model ________________________ **Year** _________ **Evaluation: 4 3 2 1**

_____ **1.** Check service information for the type of fuel injector being used.

____ Saturated

____ Peak and hold

_____ **2.** Connect a digital storage oscilloscope (DSO) or graphing multimeter (GMM) to the pulsed side of the injector. (Check service information for the color of wire used for the pulse.)

_____ **3.** Start the engine and observe the voltage waveform.

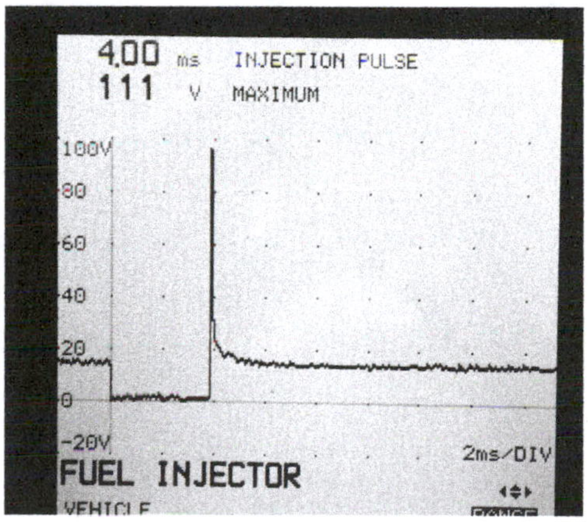
4.00 ms INJECTION PULSE
111 V MAXIMUM
100V
80
60
40
20
0
-20V
2ms/DIV
FUEL INJECTOR

_____ **4.** Does the voltage spike (kick) exceed 30 volts? _____ **Yes** _____ **No**

_____ **5.** What is the injector pulse-width? __________ (normally between 1.5 and 3.5 mS at idle on a warm engine)

_____ **6.** Based on the test performed, what is the necessary action? ____________________

____

____

Exhaust Gas Analysis

Meets NATEF Task: (A8-B-6) Prepare 4 or 5 gas analyzer; inspect and prepare vehicle for test, and obtain exhaust readings; interpret readings, and determine necessary action. (P-3)

Name ______________________ **Date** __________ **Time on Task** __________

Make/Model ______________________ **Year** __________ **Evaluation:** **4 3 2 1**

_____ **1.** Check the instruction information for the exhaust gas analyzer being used to determine the proper test procedures to follow.

____

____

_____ **2.** Check the vehicle for exhaust leaks and other faults that could affect the exhaust gas readings.

____

_____ **3.** Prepare the vehicle for testing, which usually includes operating the engine until normal operating temperature has been achieved. List other items listed by the test equipment manufacturer that should be performed.

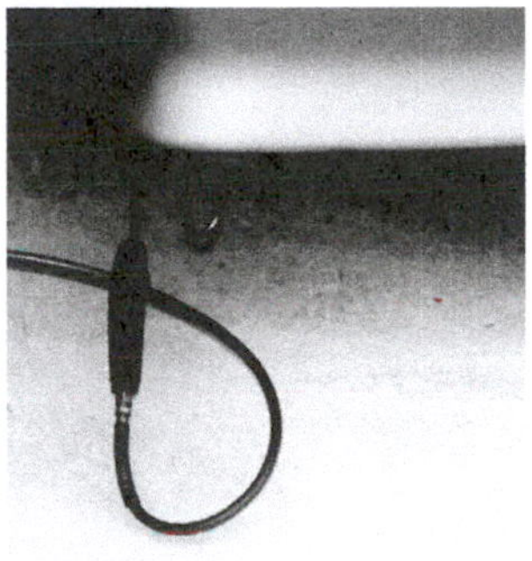

____

____

_____ **4.** Obtain the exhaust gas readings and compare them to specifications.

Gas	**Idle**	**2500 RPM**	**General Specifications**
HC			Max 50 PPM
CO			Max 0.5%
CO_2			12% to 15% or higher
O_2			0% to 2%
NO_X			Less than 100 PPM @ idle Less than 1000 PPM @ wide open throttle

_____ **5.** Based on the exhaust gas readings, what is the necessary action?

____

Diagnosis of Emission-Related Concerns

Meets NATEF Task: (A8-B-5) Diagnose the causes of emissions or driveability concerns resulting from malfunctions in the computerized engine control system with stored diagnostic trouble codes. (P-1)

Name ______________________ **Date** __________ **Time on Task** __________

Make/Model ______________________ **Year** __________ **Evaluation: 4 3 2 1**

_____ **1.** Check service information for the specified methods to follow to determine the cause of an emission-related concern with stored diagnostic trouble codes.

____

____

____

____

____

____

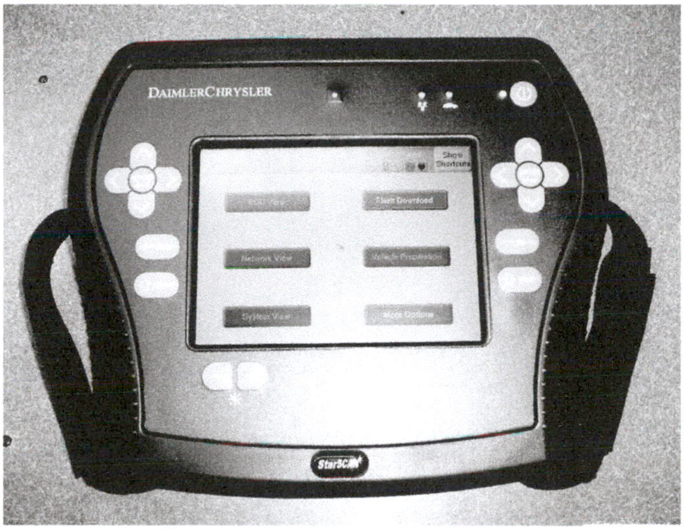
DAIMLERCHRYSLER

_____ **2.** Following the vehicle manufacturer's recommended procedure, retrieve the stored DTC(s).

DTC	Description of DTC	Possible Causes

_____ **3.** What emission concerns could result from faults indicated by the DTCs?

____

____

_____ **4.** Based on the test results and service information, what is the necessary action?

____

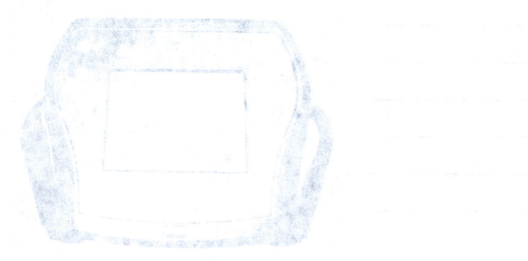

Exhaustive System Backpressure Test

Meets NATEF Task: (A8-A-5 and A8-E-4) Perform exhaust system back-pressure test; determine necessary action. (P-1)

Name ______________________________ **Date** __________ **Time on Task** __________

Make/Model ________________________ **Year** __________ **Evaluation: 4 3 2 1**

A clogged or partially restricted exhaust greatly affects engine performance. Lack of power is a common symptom of a partially restricted exhaust system. In severe cases, the engine may start/stall due to exhaust system restriction.

_____ **1.** Check service information for the specified maximum backpressure. ______________

____

_____ **2.** Remove the oxygen sensor from the exhaust manifold and install tool to measure exhaust back pressure.

NOTE: This tool can be made from an 18 mm fitting and a vacuum hose nipple.

_____ **3.** Connect a vacuum/pressure gauge to the exhaust back pressure tool. Start the engine and run at idle and observe exhaust back pressure.

______ psi back pressure (maximum allowable back pressure at idle is 1.25 psi.)

OK _____ **NOT OK** _____

_____ **4.** Operate the engine at a constant speed of 2500 RPM and observe the exhaust back pressure.

______ psi back pressure (Maximum allowable back pressure at 2500 RPM is 2.5 psi.)

OK _____ **NOT OK** _____

_____ **5.** Based on the results of the backpressure test, what is the necessary action?

____

We Support NATEF

PCV System Inspection

Meets NATEF Task: (A8-E-1, A8-E-2) Diagnose oil leaks, emissions, and driveability concerns caused by the positive crankcase ventilation (PCV) system; determine necessary action. (P-2)

Name ______________________ **Date** __________ **Time on Task** __________

Make/Model ______________________ **Year** __________ **Evaluation: 4 3 2 1**

_____ **1.** Check service information for the recommended steps to follow when testing or servicing the positive crankcase ventilation (PCV) system.

____

____

_____ **2.** Check service information and describe the location of the following:

PCV valve ______________________

Crankcase vent filter ______________________

Fixed orifice (if equipped) ______________________

Other (describe) ______________________

_____ **3.** What is specified replacement interval for the PCV valve?

____

_____ **4.** Remove and clear the PCV valve (if equipped) and note the condition.

____ Like new ____ Very dirty

____ Slightly dirty ____ Valve clogged or stuck

____ Other (describe) ______________________

_____ **5.** Based on the test and inspection and on the recommendation of the vehicle manufacturer, what is the necessary action?

____

EGR System Scan Tool Diagnosis

Meets NATEF Task: (A8-E-3) Diagnose emissions and driveability concerns caused by the exhaust gas recirculation (EGR) system; determine necessary action. (P-1)

Name ______________________ **Date** __________ **Time on Task** __________

Make/Model ______________________ **Year** __________ **Evaluation:** 4 3 2 1

_____ **1.** Check service information for the specified testing procedure of the exhaust gas recirculation (EGR) system using a scan tool.

____

____

_____ **2.** List the EGR-related data that can be retrieved using a scan tool.

____

_____ **3.** List the scan tool commands (bi-directional) for the EGR system and describe the results of the tests.

Unit Commanded	**Results**
______________	______________
______________	______________
______________	______________

_____ **4.** Has the EGR OBD II monitor run? ______________________

_____ **5.** Based on the results of the scan tool diagnosis, what is the necessary action?

____

____

____

____

____

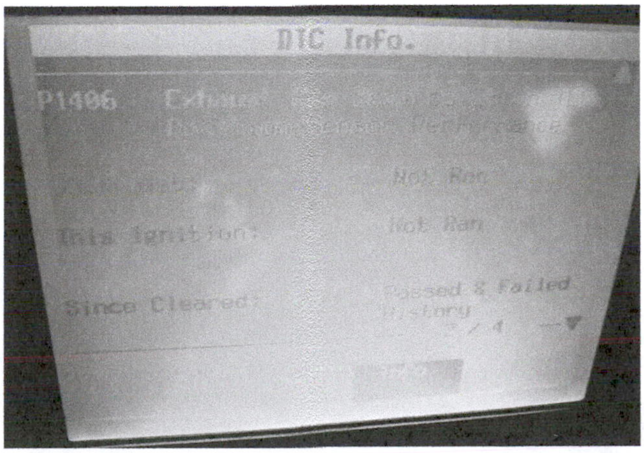
P1406
This Ignition:
Not Ran
Since Cleared:
Passed & Failed
History

Service EGR System

Meets NATEF Task: (A8-E-7) Inspect, test, service and replace components of the EGR system, exhaust passages, vacuum/pressure controls, filters and hoses; perform necessary action. (P-1)

Name ________________________ **Date** __________ **Time on Task** __________

Make/Model ________________________ **Year** _________ **Evaluation: 4 3 2 1**

The EGR passages and valve that control the flow of exhaust gases can become clogged with carbon. The EGR valve and passages may need to be cleaned if one or more of the following conditions are present.

- A computer diagnosis trouble code (DTC) indicating the lack of EGR flow
- The failure of an exhaust emission test for excessive NOx
- Excessive engine spark knock (ping or detonation)

_____ **1.** Check service information for the recommended procedures to follow when servicing the EGR system.

____

_____ **2.** What problem(s) exists? ____

_____ **3.** Remove the EGR valve and inspect for clogged passages. Clean as needed.

Valve was clogged _____ Valve was OK _____

_____ **4.** Start the engine. Exhaust should be heard and felt coming from the open passage where the EGR valve was located.

CAUTION: Be sure to wear eye protection. Particles of carbon can be forced out of the EGR passage with great force when the engine starts.

Exhaust flowed freely _____ Exhaust did not flow freely _____

_____ **5.** To clean the passages of carbon, remove the plugs or EGR valve and insert a stiff wire into an electric drill and use it to ream out the passages.

_____ **6.** Reinstall the EGR valve with a new gasket and check the engine for proper operation.

_____ **7.** What is the necessary action? ____________________

____

EGR Electrical Sensors

Meets NATEF Task: (A8-E-6) Inspect and test electrical/electronic sensors, controls, and wiring of exhaust gas recirculation (EGR) systems; perform necessary action. (P-2)

Name ______________________________ **Date** __________ **Time on Task** __________

Make/Model ________________________ **Year** _________ **Evaluation: 4 3 2 1**

_____ **1.** Check service information for the recommended tests and diagnostic procedure to follow to diagnose EGR system sensors and controls.

____

____

____

____

____

_____ **2.** List the tools and equipment needed as specified by the vehicle manufacturer. Check all that apply.

____ Scan tool

____ Vacuum pump

____ Digital multimeter (DMM)

____ 5-gas exhaust analyzer

____ Other (describe) ______________________________

_____ **3.** Based on the test results, what is the necessary action?

____

____

Catalytic Converter Test

Meets NATEF Task: (A8-E-4 and A8-E-9) Inspect and test catalytic converter efficiency. (P-2 and P1)

Name ______________________ **Date** __________ **Time on Task** __________

Make/Model ______________________ **Year** __________ **Evaluation: 4 3 2 1**

_____ **1.** Check service information for the recommended test to perform on the catalytic converter.

____

____

_____ **2.** The recommended test(s) include the following. Check all that apply.

____ Check for loose substrate (rattle noise)

____ Check temperature differences

____ Use propane

____ Use an exhaust gas analyzer

____ Other (describe) ______________________________

_____ **3.** Which tests were performed and what were the results?

a. ____________________ Result: ____________________

b. ____________________ Result: ____________________

c. ____________________ Result: ____________________

_____ **4.** Based on the tests and inspection of the catalytic converter, what is the necessary action?

____

____

Secondary Air Injection Diagnosis

Meets NATEF Task: (A8-E-4 and A8-E-8) Inspect and test mechanical components of secondary air injection systems; perform necessary action. (P-3 and P2)

Name ______________________ **Date** __________ **Time on Task** __________

Make/Model ______________________ **Year** __________ **Evaluation: 4 3 2 1**

_____ **1.** Check service information for the recommended procedures to follow when inspecting and testing the AIR pump components.

____

_____ **2.** Carefully inspect the condition of all of the hoses, check the valves and the metal lines for corrosion or damage.

_____ **3.** Start the engine and feel the air pump lines to confirm the proper air flow.

NOTE: A defective one-way check valve at the exhaust manifold can allow hot exhaust gases to flow past the check valve and cause damage to the switching valves, hoses or air pump itself. These exhaust gases can cause poor engine operation and stalling if drawn into the air intake system.

_____ **4.** Inspect the air pump drive belt for cracks and proper tension.

_____ **5.** Inspect the electrical/electronic components of the air injection system.

_____ **6.** Based on the inspection, what is the necessary action?

____

____

____

Evaporative Emission Controls Diagnosis

Meets NATEF Task: (A8-E-10) Inspect and test components and hoses of the evaporative emissions control system; perform necessary action. (P-1)

Name ______________________ **Date** __________ **Time on Task** __________

Make/Model ______________________ **Year** __________ **Evaluation: 4 3 2 1**

_____ **1.** Check service information for the specified tests and procedures to follow to diagnose the problems in the evaporative emission control system.

____

____

____

_____ **2.** List the tools and equipment specified for use by service information. Check all that apply.

____ Special tester (describe) ______________________

____ Scan tool

____ Other (describe) ______________________

_____ **3.** List the components included in the evaporative emission control unit and describe how each is to be tested according to service information.

	Component	Test or Inspection
a.	____________	____________
b.	____________	____________
c.	____________	____________
d.	____________	____________

_____ **4.** Based on the results of the tests and inspection, what is the necessary action?

____

Smoke Test of the EVAP System

Meets NATEF Task: (A8-E-5 and A8-E-10) Inspect and test components and hoses of the evaporative emissions control system and DTCs; perform necessary action. (P-1s)

Name ______________________ **Date** __________ **Time on Task** __________

Make/Model ______________________ **Year** __________ **Evaluation: 4 3 2 1**

_____ **1.** Check for any EVAP-related diagnostic trouble codes (DTCs).

____

_____ **2.** Check service information for the procedures and pressures to follow when checking the evaporative emission control system for leaks using smoke.

____

____

Specified maximum pressure = ______________________

_____ **3.** Connect the smoke machine to the evaporative emission control system following the instructions supplied with the smoke machine.

____

____

____

____

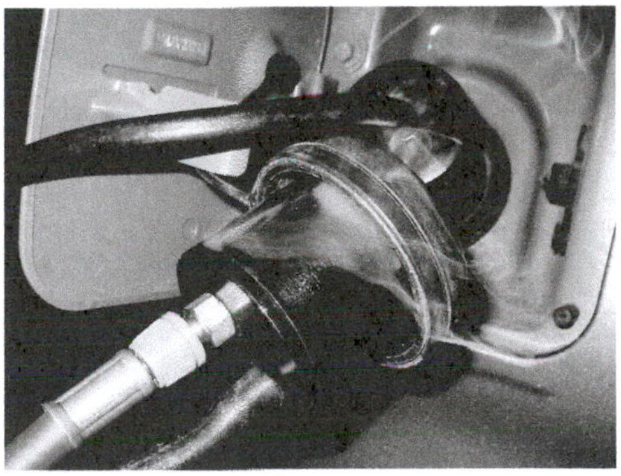

_____ **4.** Use a bright light and look for smoke leaking from the evaporative emission control system. Describe the leaks, if any.

____

____

_____ **5.** Based on the results of the scan tool and smoke testing, what is the necessary action?

____

OBD II Connector Identification

Meets NATEF Task: (A8-A-2) Locate and interpret vehicle and major component identification information. (P-1)

Name ______________________________ **Date** __________ **Time on Task** __________

Make/Model __________________________ **Year** __________ **Evaluation: 4 3 2 1**

_____ **1.** Check service information and check which cavities of the OBD II diagnostic link connector (DLC) have electrical (metal) terminals.

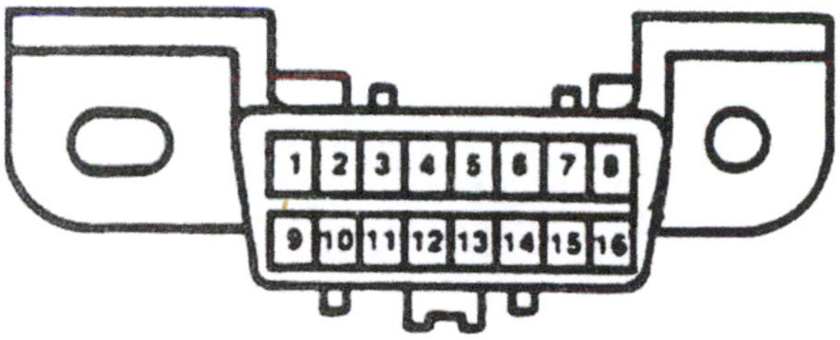
1
2
3
4
5
6
7
8
9
10
11
12
13
14
15
16

_____ **2.** Use service information and determine the identification for each of the terminals.

1. ______________________________
2. ______________________________
3. ______________________________
4. ______________________________
5. ______________________________
6. ______________________________
7. ______________________________
8. ______________________________
9. ______________________________
10. ______________________________
11. ______________________________
12. ______________________________
13. ______________________________
14. ______________________________
15. ______________________________
16. ______________________________

We Support NATEF

Scan Tool Diagnosis

Meets NATEF Task: (A8-B-2 and A8-B-3) Retrieve and record stored OBD II diagnostic trouble codes; clear codes. (P-1)

Name ______________________ **Date** __________ **Time on Task** __________

Make/Model ______________________ **Year** __________ **Evaluation: 4 3 2 1**

_____ **1.** Check service information for the specified method for retrieving diagnostic trouble codes on the OBD II vehicle being serviced.

____

____

_____ **2.** Set a diagnostic trouble code by unplugging a component that is check by the comprehensive component monitor (CCM), such as the throttle position sensor.

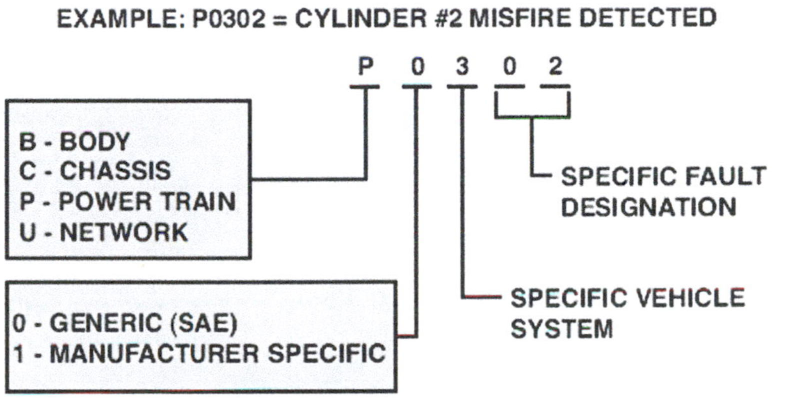
EXAMPLE: P0302 = CYLINDER #2 MISFIRE DETECTED
P 0 3 0 2
B - BODY
C - CHASSIS
P - POWER TRAIN
U - NETWORK
0 - GENERIC (SAE)
1 - MANUFACTURER SPECIFIC
SPECIFIC FAULT DESIGNATION
SPECIFIC VEHICLE SYSTEM

_____ **3.** Retrieve and record the stored diagnostic trouble code (DTC).

Which code(s) was set? ____

_____ **4.** Check the service information for the specified method to use to erase (clear) the DTCs.

____

_____ **5.** Erase (clear the DTCs).

_____ **6.** Verify that the DTC has been cleared.

Hybrid Vehicle HV Circuit Disconnect

Meets NATEF Task: (A6-B-7) Identify location of hybrid vehicle high-voltage circuit disconnect (service plug) location and safety precautions. (P-3)

Name ______________________ **Date** __________ **Time on Task** __________

Make/Model ______________________ **Year** __________ **Evaluation: 4 3 2 1**

_____ **1.** Check service information for the location of the high-voltage disconnect (service plug) for the following hybrid electric vehicles:

Toyota Prius ____________________

____

Toyota Camry hybrid ____________________

____

Honda Civic and Accord hybrid ______

____

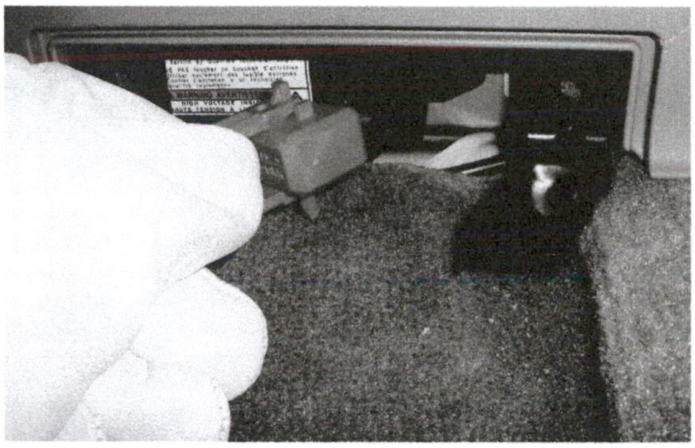

Ford/Mercury hybrid ____________________

General Motors PHT hybrid ____________________

General Motors two-mode hybrid ____________________

Saturn hybrid ____________________

Other (describe) ____________________

_____ **2.** Check service information and list the safety precautions specified when de-powering the high-voltage circuits.

____

____

____

We Support NATEF

Identify HV of Hybrid Electric Vehicles

Meets NATEF Task: (A6-B-7) Identify high-voltage circuits of hybrid electric vehicles and related safety precautions. (P-3)

Name ______________________ **Date** __________ **Time on Task** __________

Make/Model ______________________ **Year** __________ **Evaluation: 4 3 2 1**

_____ **1.** Check service information for how to identify the high-voltage circuits which are covered with orange conduit and can be located anywhere in the vehicle. Check all that apply.

____ Orange high-voltage cables visible underneath the vehicle (describe the location) ______________________________

____ Orange high-voltage cables under the hood (describe the location and components) ______________________________

____

____ Orange cables in the trunk or rear area of the vehicle (describe the location and components) ______________________________

____

_____ **2.** Check service information and list the safety precautions regarding the high-voltage circuits.

____

____

____

____

____

____

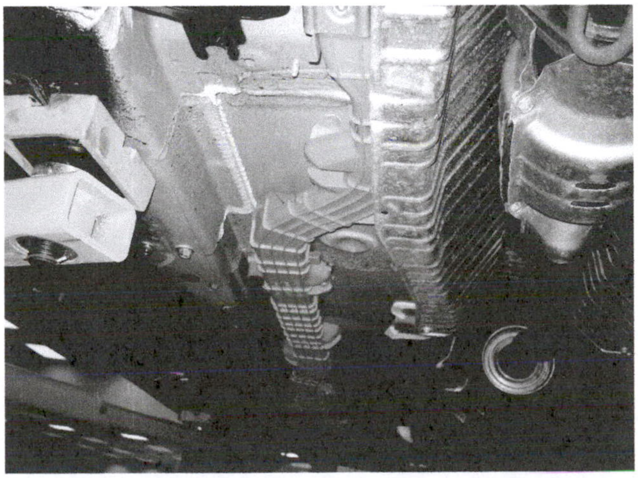

We Support NATEF

Electric/Fuel Cell Vehicle Identification

Meets NATEF Task: (A6-B-7) Identify high-voltage circuits of electric vehicles and related safety precautions. (P-3)

Name ______________________ **Date** __________ **Time on Task** __________

Make/Model ______________________ **Year** __________ **Evaluation:** 4 3 2 1

_____ **1.** Search service information for information on electric vehicles.

	Brand/Model	Type of Batteries	Voltage	Charging Method
A.				
B.				
C.				
D.				
E.				

ELECTRIC
VEHICLE
PARKING
ONLY

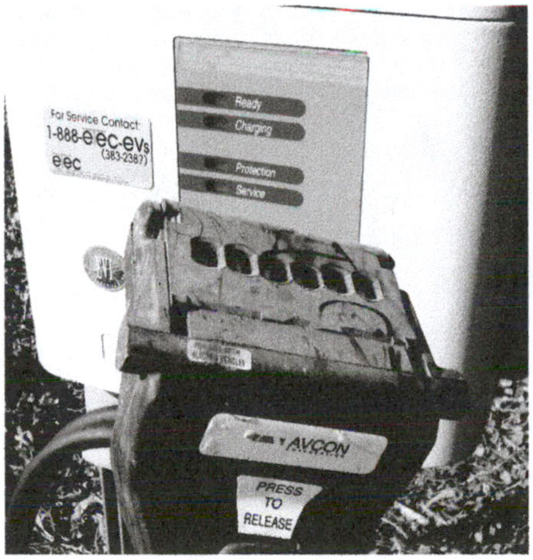
For Service Contact:
1-888-eec-eVs
(383-2387)
eec
Ready
Charging
Protection
Service
AVCON
PRESS
TO
RELEASE

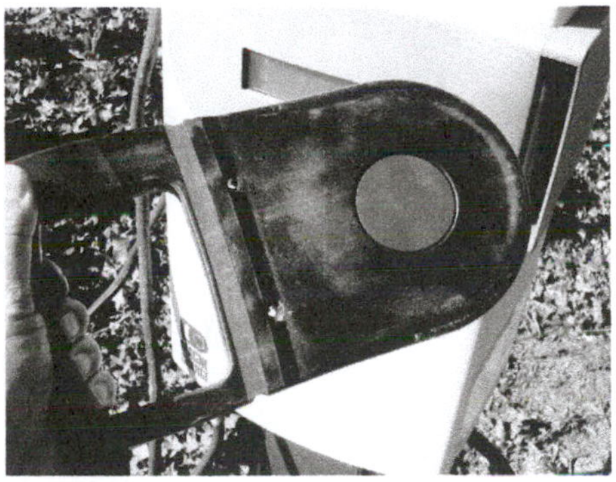

_____ **2.** Check service information for related safety precautions.

____

____